On the Move

Cover design by mixx design www.mixxdesign.com

Note for Librarians: a cataloguing record for this book that includes Dewey Decimal
Classification and US Library of Congress numbers is available from the Library and
Archives of Canada. The complete cataloguing record can be obtained from their online
database at:
www.collectionscanada.ca/amicus/index-e.html
ISBN 1-4120-4708-0

TRAFFORD

Offices in Canada, USA, Ireland, UK and Spain
This book was published *on-demand* in cooperation with Trafford Publishing. On-demand
publishing is a unique process and service of making a book available for retail sale to the
public taking advantage of on-demand manufacturing and Internet marketing. On-demand
publishing includes promotions, retail sales, manufacturing, order fulfilment, accounting and
collecting royalties on behalf of the author.
Book sales for North America and international:
Trafford Publishing, 6E–2333 Government St.,
Victoria, BC v8t 4p4 CANADA
phone 250 383 6864 (toll-free 1 888 232 4444)
fax 250 383 6804; email to orders@trafford.com
Book sales in Europe:
Trafford Publishing (uk) Ltd., Enterprise House, Wistaston Road Business Centre,
Wistaston Road, Crewe, Cheshire cw2 7rp UNITED KINGDOM
phone 01270 251 396 (local rate 0845 230 9601)
facsimile 01270 254 983; orders.uk@trafford.com
Order online at:
www.trafford.com/robots/04-2516.html

10 9 8 7 6 5 4 3 2

Dedication
To my husband and children.
Thanks for the adventure!

Author's note

I am an Australian. (Please do not stop reading!) Currently abroad with my family, I have learned a lot through the many moves we have made. Some have been with short notice. There was little time to stress, as we filled our time with all the tasks that needed to be completed.

Moving as a single person or a couple is busy as you work and plan the move at the same time. However, you are able to be more liberal in your decisions. As adults, eating out and staying in Motel accommodation can feel more like a holiday than a transition.

When there are children to consider (from unborn to teenage,) definite planning is important. Children need security and their behaviour can vary widely as they try to make sense of the chaos.

At a new location you may find fresh scenery, an unfamiliar accent or language and possibly driving on the 'wrong' side of the road! However amongst all of this, there is a general list of processes to be completed. You still have to find the food and clothing shops, connect the electricity, gas and telephone and find your way to work or school.

Throughout this book, I have tried to keep the terminology as 'neutral' as possible. Depending on where in the World you are reading this collection of words, there will be differences.

For example, some will know a flashlight to be a torch; a State to mean Province; the garbage bin to the Trash can and the toilet to be the washroom or W.C.
The concept being conveyed is the same and I am sure you will be able to accept the idea being presented and adapt it to your personal situation.

The examples provided within these pages are from real life. Use our experiences to fore think potential problems.

Moving is a big event in anyone's life. It invokes change and upheaval. Make use of this time to fine tune those areas of your life that you have wanted to modify.

I hope that you find the information useful. Everybody's house has its own challenges. The topics covered are a starting point for your thoughts. You may find others as you become more focused.

I wish you a smooth transition and look forward to hearing from you.

Acknowledgements

To Nan, Grandad and Michel.

You have given us endless support with meals, childcare and guidance when sorting out what to pack. You have been there to move countless boxes from one room to the next or to be a sounding board to vent against when all seemed to be going wrong. I appreciate all that you have done, and hope to return the favour when the shoe is on the other foot.

Friends, too, have helped in our endeavours for a new address, from providing extra hands and driving vehicles, to giving us somewhere to drop off suitcases or provide local knowledge.

Moves were made intrastate, interstate and overseas with the help of Removalist companies. The information kits provided were very useful. I am grateful for the ideas provided. Thanks for not laughing too loudly as you packed our belongings! At times I could see that you wanted to ask a question. Your professionalism prevented you from doing so.

I have gleaned information and helpful hints too, from observing others in their endeavour for a new address.

Thanks to Audrey, Lorelie and Diana for their assistance. Their patience in reading through these words and enthusiastic encouragement, have helped to keep my dream alive!

P.S Advance apologies to Uncle Arthur and Aunt Molly!

Table of Contents

Introduction

Why people move house

A question: If you had to leave your home with five minutes notice, could you put your hands on your most important possessions? What about in ten minutes or even an hour? Would this give you enough time to think where you left that photo album or treasured memento?

__Activity One__: Sit down now and make a list of what you would include for each time frame. (Only give yourself five, ten and sixty minutes respectively to compile them.) Keep them handy for later. (If you cannot think of what is in the cupboards, maybe this activity will pique your curiosity to find out!)

Why did you pick up this book? Are you or someone you know thinking of moving? Do you want to separate the junk from the treasure, but are not sure where to start?

As you watch the news and see the latest natural disaster to befall a city or town, do you ever stop to think how you would cope with such a situation?

Everyday, people leave their homes. They go to work, the shops, to visit friends or for a walk. They return as usual and think nothing of it. Others are forced to leave, by natural disaster or a security threat; (a gas leak, a flood or fire.) They have little information on what is happening and when they will be able to return.

If **you** had to leave in a hurry, how would you feel? Could you think clearly enough to pick up those items you would need, to live normally for an extended period of time, away from your home?

The main aim of clearing the excess is to find out which possessions are important to you. It makes no difference whether you are actually leaving your residence or not, the point is you have thought about such an event and have prepared for it. By considering the scenario in advance, you reduce the stress.

This book will encourage you to explore those dark cupboards and unearth long forgotten riches! (It is your 'silent partner' in the adventure!) There is no doubt that the task can be huge. You will ponder why you hoarded stuff in the first place. Did the job of clearing out get too big and now you don't know where to start? Do you like to have 'things' around you? No time to spend sorting what is what? Are you holding onto this 'undefined wealth' because it was given to you by someone in the family and you do not want to offend them?

Western culture is materialistic. We do not live from day to day with items found to hand. We buy and consume new products on a regular basis. This is not a fault, but a necessity to ensure that the economy continues to function. The problem comes when we start to retain EVERYTHING that comes into our house, 'Just in case I need it later!'

Some people joke: 'The person with the most possessions at the end wins.' I would counter: 'Remove some of the clutter and allow yourself to experience more options the world has to offer.'

Many of life's best experiences are found in a single moment in time and cost nothing.

Look around you now. Are there newspapers, mail or clothing just hanging around? Is it because you have nowhere to put them or were you just waiting for the right time to get back to them?

From an insurance point of view, (assuming you have a current policy,) if the worst happened, you are covered for the basics. This is basic furniture and bedding, kitchenware and accessories.
Imagine bare furniture. No picture frames on the walls and no ornaments sitting on tables.

Think of those special items you have collected through the years. Can you name twelve of them without looking? A house is not a home without these more personal items that define you and your family.
They decorate the space with memories.

BUT:

If you had the opportunity to replace them, would you look for something similar or a whole new style?

For those about to change address, consider these possibilities.

Short moves are within the same city. You may move many of the smaller items in numerous car trips. Think of the time saved if you were to only move the important stuff.

Long Distance moves mean major change. They can be temporary or permanent. You may not be allowed to take all of your possessions with you. Some may need to go into storage.

If moving for work, a company may restrict the volume of goods they are prepared to pay for. The size of your family, the location to which you are going and the duration of your placement are all considerations to keep in mind.

Think about the cost of storage. Sentimentality aside, are your possessions really worth the expense? If your fridge is really old, would it be better to sell it now and buy another when you return? Will your children have out grown their beds – the pink frills of a nine year old may not be fitting for a budding teenager! Will their toys still suit them?

Some people will prefer to take **everything** with them, and sort it out as they unpack. This can be false economy. The rush to get things squared away in the new house may mean that **no** sorting occurs at all! The empty space envisioned will be filled with 'junk' and you are back to square one.

Today is the day! You need a plan.

The De-clutter Process

If you want to sort your treasures simply to take stock of where you are, then you can take as long as you like – but I suggest that this course of action take no more than one month in total. The problem with hoarding is that you can always say that it is a work in progress!

If, however, you plan to move, then you need to start this process as soon as possible.

Relocating is well regarded as one of the most stressful things that a person can do in their lifetime. However with careful planning, you can reduce the tension. How busy you are going to be, will depend on how soon you have to move.

Many people look around their home and say that they dread the thought. They have been in their home for many years, the cupboards are full, not to mention the basement, attic or garage spaces!

Change your focus. Rather than seeing a hassle; consider it as a chance to start fresh. Think about why you have a house the size it is. Did you need to take on such a place just to accommodate these riches? Own up, did you need to build a spare shed, or take the car out of the garage or lose a bedroom just to store them?

By removing some of the clutter, you widen your housing options. Streamlining will allow your house to better reflect your current lifestyle choice. Housekeeping duties will take less effort and time. More of your day can be used to go for a walk, make some new friends or just catch up on rereading those favourite books you thought were lost. They were in fact, hidden behind Uncle Arthur's old pile of newspapers!

Activity Two:

What's your home like? When did **you** last look into the spare bedroom? Do you **know** what is lurking in there? Go and have a look now. **Don't touch anything.** I'll wait until you get back before we continue...

You're back! What did you find? Could you see what was hidden right in the back behind the old blankets and photo frames?
Let's get started!

One of the first lessons to success is to know what you have in the first place!

Sorting out the chaos

Word of warning:

Before you start sticking your hands into dark crevices and dusty spaces, be aware that some little creature may have decided to make it their home first!! A torch or other directed lighting will be useful, as well as a poker to give the creature advance warning of your invasion! Most should be harmless, but the fright value may be enough to put you off the task quicker than finding an old pair of running shoes that 'died' long ago!!

As the proverb says, 'A daunting task is best broken down into the smallest portions.' The process of sorting is best done by two people. One who will make the decisions and a helper (emotions neutral!) to put each object into its appropriate pile.

Super Luck Box

Find a small box, (a shoe box would be great) and label it '**Super Luck Box**'. Into this, place any odd article you find. For example, a piece of a jigsaw puzzle or game and odd socks! Throw in the sticky tape, stapler, glue, writing implement, marking pens and pieces of notepaper or labels – anything that you will need to sort out the chaos. They always seem to go missing just when you need them. Remember to return them to the box each time you use them.

You will need some sturdy boxes to hold papers. For now, label them (on the inside) as your '**Essentials**' boxes. You may need more than one, so that they are not too heavy to carry. Put them with your filing system until you are ready to tackle this project.

You need to make space for three different categories of items. Make labels that read: 'Long Store', 'Selling' and 'Living'. You will also need garbage bags or a place for Rubbish.

These labels **roughly** divide your possessions. There is more to do within every group later. This process will reduce the number of times you have to make decisions about each treasure.

Label the spaces **clearly**, so you do not sell the family heirlooms instead of the old pile of newspapers that Uncle Arthur or you had hoped to read one day!

Wardrobes in separate rooms are ideal. Put a label on each and fill them respectively with the items of a category. Later, when you need to look at the goods to be sold, you will go straight to the 'Selling' space and finalise those items. No stress – lots of time saved and no new clutter!

Starting small

Start with a cupboard that you use all the time. You are familiar with most of its contents and are used to opening and closing the door! By the time you get to the least opened space in your house, you will be brimming with confidence to deal with any surprises!

Lay all the contents of one shelf out on empty table; preferably away from the space where it was previously housed. The focus has to be on the **object** itself, rather than how well it coordinates with other items of décor.

First impressions are very important here.

If, your initial reaction is:
a) Cringe
b) You shriek: 'what's this?!'
c) The second person wants to use it for target practice;
   then it is time to remove it from your inventory!

You need to be strict about this process.

As you examine each item, have a good look at it.
* Do you like it?
* Can you still use it?
* Is it in good condition?

As you get accustomed to the de-clutter process, you will become more objective about each possession. Your self-control will make you question more often, whether you really need to keep or buy an item.

The more time that a piece remains in your hand,
the less chance you have of getting rid of it!

How are you going? If you have managed to clear out the whole closet in one effort, you deserve a break! Find a relaxing activity to celebrate the great work you have completed.

When you come back, you can decide to:

>   a) Leave the next cupboard for tomorrow (time
>   permitting) – don't forget you now have areas of
>   the house tied up as 'holding pens'!

Or

>   b) Attack that next area with your new found
>   enthusiasm!

See you soon!

The Filing Cabinet - Do you know what is inside?

Bring out your 'Essentials' boxes. **When complete, they will need to be securely stored; but accessible quickly.**

Protect yourself against 'Identity theft.' Do not mark them as 'Important papers.' They need to blend in with their surroundings, yet able to be removed by the right people quickly. They will enable you to include paper and computer records in your emergency plan no matter how short notice.

Which papers?

Start with the first file in your filing system. Look at each paper carefully. You are looking for those papers that define your life.
Include a copy and policy information (preferably the latest) relating to:

- Bank and credit card statements
- Finance companies and Lay bys
- Insurance policies – (Vehicle, Income and Personal, House and Contents)
- Mortgage Documents
- Warranties
- House Deeds and plans
- Birth, Death and Marriage certificates
- Resume and education certificates
- Medical records and X-rays
- Tax records
- Passports
- Health care and Child benefit numbers
- Cheque books and important receipts
- Memberships for clubs and 'points' programmes
- Lottery tickets that need to be checked
- Change of address list (to be compiled)
- Voting card
- Valuation certificates
- Share Certificates and other financial documents
- A record of credit card and other reference numbers. Remember – **NO PASSWORDS**.

Make a list of each Company or Organisation you come across for your 'Change of Address' list. An address book can be used if compiling by hand or a computer spreadsheet can be filled in. (Just remember to save it to disk and print off a copy.)

The list will need to be amended from time to time. Note the contact address for changing details. (Some of these will be able to be done over the internet. Others require you to make these changes in person or in writing.) Make a list of friends and family too.

Note internet addresses of companies and friends. Don't overlook bills, important notices, old employers and Retirement funds. You will need to ensure final group certificates for tax returns and information regarding future investment decisions find you at your new address.

These items are not of monetary value, but make the process of starting over a little more structured.

Certificates and policies and the like, can usually be replaced (although sometimes at cost.) The official copies are hopefully safely stored and available at any time. If you can protect <u>your</u> copy, you will be a step in front of many others.

Without it, you will need to ring around (sometimes interstate or overseas,) to arrange replacements. Your time will be spent explaining to strangers that, 'you have lost your possessions, certificates and warranties. Could they process your request without them?'
With these vital records on hand, you can quote the relevant reference number and get on with your claim.

It can be difficult to keep these boxes just for papers. Special photographs of friends and family and treasured possessions have a tendency to slip in. Try to keep them for their real purpose, and store other most valuable items, for example, photograph albums nearby.

This system is not foolproof – you or someone you trust must know where the boxes are and be able to get to them in an urgent situation. Their value comes in part; from knowing you have reduced the number of situations for which you are not prepared.

Find the lists you made earlier. Are you surprised at what you thought to include on each? When you are under pressure, it is easy to overlook items that may be important.

With your boxes prepared, **rewrite the lists**. Use different, brightly coloured paper for each to give your senses a lift. This will help you to focus on the task.

Include the boxes in the five minute list. For the important items that cannot be stored near your essential boxes, mark on the list their location.

In a calm manner, move from room to room. Your brain will process the relative importance of the items you see.

Here are some suggestions:

Five minutes –
 • House/Car Keys
 • Wallet or purse
 • Coat or Jacket
 • Any essential medicines
 • All family members (including pets)
 • Your Essentials Boxes
 • Snack foods –(fruit, packets of biscuits, cereal, water bottle)

Ten minutes –
 • all the above
 • A favourite toy for each child
 • Photo album or family memento, (if you know **exactly** where it is!)

One hour –
 • all the above
 • Change/s of clothing for each household member
 • More food and water (for pets too!)
 • Torch and radio (battery power or wind up)
 • First aid kit
 • Toiletries and medical supplies
 • Extra toys or activities to pass waiting time
 • Some family memorabilia
 • School or work books/manuals and uniforms
 • A tool kit

Stick the lists inside the lids of your boxes. They are now readily available should the need to use them ever arise.
Your new resource will assist greatly should you be forced to stay away from your home indefinitely.

Your mind won't spin as you try to decide '**NOW!**' what to take – amidst noise, sirens, children crying and people shouting orders. Your heart won't need to race as you calmly gather the bits and pieces that you have already decided upon.

Make sure that all capable members of your family know where the boxes are. Include them in your house escape plan so that valuable time is not lost through misunderstanding.
You need to revise the boxes regularly so that they remain a living record.

Okay, what about the rest of your papers? Check with your Accountant or the Taxation Department to see how many years your records have to cover. At some time in the future an audit may be applied to your affairs.

If your filing system is small, a portable folder with many pockets may be sufficient.

If you have sold a lawn mower sometime ago, you do not need to keep the service manual. (Preferably you have handed it onto the new owner!) Furniture and home appliance receipts really have no value – if the item is now well used or of age, unless kept for historical significance. Insurance 'refunds' are based on current values and often will bear no resemblance to what you originally paid. Old credit card advertising and <u>very old</u> statements - as long as you have reconciled them with receipts; can also be discarded.

Six months before your income tax needs to be filed, go through your papers. Create a file or use a large envelope to hold any receipts and records you will be able to use in lodging your assessment. Add new papers as they arrive.
After your tax return has been filed, go through your system again and remove all papers for the year just past. Label a set of envelopes or folders and file these papers.

It will be more efficient to browse one year's worth of paper, rather than the last five when you need to find an important receipt.
Make note of any previous addresses and old credit card or bank account numbers (and what name/s they were held in.) This is a handy record to verify your past credit history! It may be useful for gas, electricity and telephone connection deposits.

Disposing of old papers that contain personal information needs careful consideration. Throwing them into the garbage may compromise your personal privacy. Borrow a shredder or find other suitable means to destroy these documents properly.

Family Heirlooms

These are tricky! They have been handed down from one generation to another. You have been storing them for a **long** time. What **do** you **do** with them? Are they items that you would like to display? Is there someone who you would like to hand them on to? (If not now, then are they mentioned in your Will specifically?)

I am not advocating you just throw out the family memories to make space. Just that you have a closer look at what is lurking in that cupboard or wardrobe and determine whether it is important to **you**. Some of those items may be significant treasures. For example films, photographs, clothing and works of art or memorabilia that need specialised preservation. Would a Museum restore them to a suitable condition for display in their gallery? It may give you piece of mind to see that they are properly cared for. Others may then experience a sample of the past, through items that have given you and your family great pride through the years.

It may also reduce your insurance premiums if they had been previously listed – or were they?! If you have items separately listed, when did you last have them valued?

Activity Three:
As you find each family piece, think about what makes it special.

Has it been kept because it belonged to a favourite relative? If they are still alive, when did you last visit them? Would you gain the same sense of comfort visiting a retirement home and talking with others who lived through their era? (The residents will enjoy the company, and you may gain a new friend or two!)

Have you held onto a relic of your past because it reminds you of a long ago holiday? When were you last there? Has it changed? Could you create new family memories by holidaying there again? Explain to your family why the area is special to you. They will appreciate a sense of belonging to an even greater family unit that encompasses not just the moment but a place of time.

If the item is kept just because you like it, consider if it clashes with your other possessions. With enough items in this style you could change the look of a room from one season to another. Otherwise, you may want to display them in a special space that shows them off at their best.

If you choose to remove them from your inventory, investigate shops that sell similar items. Specialist auctions may also be an option if the piece is of great value. Do your research, but do not reveal too much information about your address in the process. You do not want to advertise where the goods are stored.

Clothing

We all have those fashion mistakes and clothes we thought would be 'in' again one day. Time to start anew! Part of your new life may be to change your shape with improved health habits!

Get rid of some of the excess - you will make room for new purchases and store remaining clothing less crushed.

If you find clothing stashed in a cupboard, first work out whose it is! If they no longer live in the house, decide if someone you know could make use of it. Make a pile for each person to whom the items are going. For anything left over put it in 'Selling'. Start with the oldest child and work your way down. Spend some time with them individually checking what still fits; what is worn out and which pieces they really do not like to wear (unless you force them to!) The handoffs could be worn around the house. It is a good time to acknowledge that little Johnny or Suzie has moved out of one phase of childhood into another.

Move any excess clothing to the 'Selling' place. Some old natural fibre clothes can be bundled up and sold as rags. (Cloth nappies make great cleaning cloths or garage/shed hand wipes!)

Now for the 'marital' wardrobe! Do not assume that just because you do not like your spouse/partner's favourite bathrobe that you can throw it out! Make sure you let them have a significant say in this process! However, if they refuse to help go through their space, then after two warnings, all bets are off! The job needs to be done.

Have a really good look at each piece in its own right.

Questions to help you:

- Do you like it?
- It may fit, but does it flatter?
- Can you match or make up an outfit?
- How often do you wear it, has your style changed?

Have a good look at your accessories,

- Are your handbags/ earrings in good repair?
- How many of them do you actually use?
- If they were handed down from other people, would they be offended if you no longer had them – be honest; do not use this as an excuse to keep them all!
- Are they a classic style that you will be able to use for special occasions?
- Are sets complete?
- Are they family heirlooms?
- Shoes - could you dance all night in them?
- Do their colours suit the outfits in your wardrobe or your other accessories?
- Does that hat compliment your hairstyle?
- Are you simply tired of wearing the same things?

If you are pregnant, the rules of what to keep can be relaxed. Knowing that your condition is a temporary one, you can keep more for **now.** However, it still would be a good idea to take stock – what has not been worn for some time, probably will not be worn once your shape returns to normal! Go through your wardrobe again at a later date to fine tune.

As you add clothes and accessories to the selling pile, consider if they can be used for a 'dress up box'. (If your brood is past this stage, preschools and day care centres appreciate donations!) Children love a variety of costumes; it might keep them occupied whilst you get another task done – like take a short break!

The Bathroom Cabinet

When did you last check what was lurking amongst the talcum powder and soaps? What medicines belonged to Uncle Arthur – even though he no longer lives with you?

If you have been on various medications for a while, when were you last reassessed? As your health improves, your medicinal needs may change! Look for those medicines (both prescription and general) outside their expiry date or are no longer being used. Bundle them up and take them to your nearest chemist.

DO NOT flush them down the toilet. The environment will suffer as the concentration of chemicals kills plant and animal life as the residues make their way to treatment works and beyond. Indeed septic tanks can be damaged if antibacterial agents are put through them. The microbes that help to break down the waste can be eliminated and the processes can stop! The odour that now emanates and the service call now needed should be lessons to stop you doing it again!

Tablets and pills must not be put into the garbage bin! They can pose a health risk to children who can mistake them for sweets.

The Book Shelf

Each book and magazine needs these considerations:

- What condition is it in?
- Do you look at the book often?
- Is it valuable? (It may require special mention when packing)
- Are later editions more useful?
- Is updated information available elsewhere? For example at a Library or on the internet.

A few books on many topics makes more interesting browsing than a whole shelf on one subject. Visitors often have different tastes to yours. This does not mean, however, that every issue of every magazine is worth keeping! One or two issues may be sufficient depending on the subject matter.

Put into the selling pile those to be discarded. Books do not usually bring a lot of money second hand.

Second hand book stores may take some from you.
Hostels (whether youth or age), prisons, hospitals and other places where groups

of people meet appreciate donations. With tight budgets, reading materials are not always able to be a high priority. As people pass through, books can change hands many times. They are picked up at one location and dropped off at another. A mobile library of sorts!

Limited editions and Historical records, however, need specialist advice if you want to dispose of them.

Remember that when books are packed, **boxes get heavy very quickly.** You will need to balance the weight of the books with other items much lighter in nature.

Think carefully about where you are going. Books can suffer when changes in temperature and humidity happen too quickly. If you are going somewhere more tropical for only a limited time, consider if the books are worth risking. Putting them into storage can also be a concern. You need to weigh up the importance of your reference collection.

[Musical instruments can be temperamental in much the same way as books. Humidity, storage or infrequent use, can play (excuse the pun!) havoc with them. You may need specialist advice to determine the best course of action.]

The Kitchen

Open all the cupboards and storage nooks in your kitchen area. Goodness, what an awful lot of gadgets! How many of them do you actually use?

Label the cupboards as 'Selling, 'Long store' and 'Living' and bring a rubbish bag.

Put all your everyday crockery, cups, glasses, cutlery and cooking utensils into the 'Living' cupboard. Saucepans and baking trays can also go into this area.

Now consider what remains.

Start at one end, and go through each shelf.

Some questions to help decide what to keep:

- Do you like it?
- Is it chipped or a handle missing?
- Have you ever used it?
- Is the instruction book with it?

- Do you have another one?
- Is it a treasured memento from someone special?
- Do they still make them (is it an antique)?
- Is there now a better product on the market?

Decide the fate of each piece as you hand it to your helper. Do not linger over that green china bowl given to you by your favourite aunt, lain forgotten on the top shelf gathering dust, waiting for the 'right' occasion that has never come up!

No one is suggesting that you go back to a Spartan existence. Serving plates and special glasses are always a handy thing to have. They add colour to a table and dress up an occasion. The sale of your excess goods will enable you to buy a display cabinet in which to show off the more pretty pieces. They can be used as required for functions and provide a colourful display at quieter times.

If the clean out is due to an International move, do not place all those duplicate items into the 'Selling' pile just yet. Make a separate spot and call it 'Settling Kit' – (See below.)

The Settling Kit – (if required)

If you are moving overseas for a limited term, some belongings will stay in storage. Think ahead to when you come back.

Initially upon return, your accommodation will be temporary until you can find a permanent home. The boxes you took with you, may take many weeks to arrive if shipping by sea. In the meantime you have a life to lead.

For differences in power supply, electrical goods should stay at home. Decide if it would be better to leave your everyday crockery, cutlery and saucepans at home too, and then buy new at your destination. This will reduce the risk of breakages and allow you to go shopping!

Aim to leave behind one set of sheets, towels and bathroom linen, blankets and dishcloths to get you started. More can be bought on your return, or simply persevere until the shipment arrives.

As your 'Settling Kit' is being packed for storage, take note of which boxes are used. Mark these distinctly as '**to be opened first**'.

Alternatively, check the phone book for 'Hire' companies. Enquire if they have a 'Settling Kit'. Friends and family may lend or the local charity shops sell basic items to get you started once again.

Children's Treasures

Always a contentious issue! The age of your children will determine how much pruning can be done.

First of all, put to one side all those items that are considered favourite and those that are used often. Make sure that all the pieces of the set/game/puzzle are accounted for. (Have a look in your **Super Luck Box** for any pieces that may have been found earlier.) If there are still pieces missing, decide if the toy is still useful. If so, keep it. If not then OUT it goes! (Someone else may need spare parts for the same set.)

Check for those old tissues, sandwich crusts and other surprises that never made it to the garbage bin. Keep a large rubbish bag handy for aforementioned items and broken toys.

With the pile left over, let the children help. You will be able to gauge their opinion of a game and if it is worth holding on to. If they decide, there will be fewer tears. You get the final say, to ensure that all those books, and other more expensive toy sets stay in the household.

(Sometimes the suggestion that they get to keep a proportion of the sale proceeds of the 'selling' toys helps!) If your children simply like to watch /play with computer games, then the job is all yours. Often, children forget what toys they have simply because they are at the bottom of the toy box. Bringing them to the surface will rekindle a spark of interest – for one day anyway!
What about all those beautiful pieces of art work the children created for you?

Ways to store Paper Art work long term

1) Fold in half, a piece of cardboard (twice the size of the largest art work) and then sew, by hand or machine the two short sides to create a pocket. The children can decorate. Ask their help to sort which pictures form part of their portfolio. Put the year and artist name on each. Place these items inside the pocket and then wrap it in a garbage bag. This should preserve them for years to come; and keep out, hopefully, the little crawlies that might find them an interesting diet! If an artwork contains food or plant materials, they cannot be stored. They attract the bugs you were trying to avoid in the first place!

2) Find a special picture frame, (get somebody else to look in the shops for you!), that allows you to store about 10 pieces of paper inside. Then you can change the picture displayed simply by reshuffling the papers within. Try Craft, Photo supplies or large department stores.

3) Place a dark sheet of fabric on the ground, and then place the artwork on it. Take pictures.

If you have multiple places to store items, divide these works of art.
Store each lot in different locations, to avoid a total loss,
should a disaster happen!

Craft and Hobby materials

First of all, try to remember how long you have had the materials in your possession. Have they been useful or just added to from each garage and shop sale? I know, you were planning to create a masterpiece, but work, the children, household chores and social life got in the way. Do you still want to create your original idea or have your talents been pushing you in another direction?

Tools can stay. They are often expensive and craftsmanship in quality tools is hard to replace. However, if you no longer intend to continue with that hobby or can share resources with someone else, then perhaps they can go too.

Sewing fabric, sequins, pieces of scrap timber, odds and ends tend to multiply all by themselves when left undisturbed for some time. Look at each piece separately. If, when you pick it up, you cannot sense what it wants to become, put it in the 'Selling' pile.

Wow, haven't you accomplished a lot already? You have now been through the worst of the rooms – I know, the garage/shed/basement is still waiting – you will need some help with this one. Nominate a day just for this project. The thought of free time (for a game of golf!) once it is completed may encourage your 'Viking spirit' – that is to be ruthless and act swiftly!

Plants and Trees

If you plan to take any established plants from the garden to your new location (within the same State,) then you need to plan for this as early as possible.

- Can you take cuttings?
- Can they cope with stress?
- Are the soil types compatible?

- Is the weather favourable for the selection of plant? For example is your particular Rose variety suited to earlier or longer periods of frost or cold? You would do better to start with a selection available from the local nursery at your new location.
- What will replace these specimens in your old garden – leaving big holes in the front lawn does little for street appeal!

If you are moving out of the State, you need to check if you are **allowed** to take them. Quarantine Services work very hard to ensure that pests and diseases are kept out of key agricultural regions. Some plants act as carriers.

Plants in pots can be added to your sale catalogue. Some will sell better in smaller sizes rather than one big pot. Make sure that they are healthy (sick plants spread disease from one yard to another.)
If they do not sell, consider donating them. Retirement villages may have avid gardeners amongst their community, who would derive great pleasure from some greenery to admire out of their window.

Roof space and under the house

When did you last check in the roof space or under the house? Might you or a previous owner have put something there long ago? Your 'enthusiastic' helper is invaluable here! A sturdy ladder, good lighting and protective clothing are all necessities.

Watch out for little crawlies, as these are their favourite haunts. Pick a cool time of day as the roof space can heat up very quickly.
Bring the pot of gold out from its hiding space.
Go and have a good wash to remove the cobwebs, dust and dirt that are tangled in your hair!

The Garage, Shed or Basement

Take a look at those projects you hoped to build or finish.

- Do you still want to build it?
- Can you use the finished project at your new location?
- Will you have time and space to complete it there?

Arm yourself with different coloured tags or pieces of chalk to mark items. Mark each pile **clearly** so that the right goods end up at the rubbish dump! Don't forget those creepy crawlies!

If it definitely is not rubbish, but you are still not sure about your ambition for a project, put it with the 'Selling' pile. If it gets sold, you can buy a new project later. If not, then it was meant for you to finish after all!

Try to sell all those tins of paint that are half full and still in good condition. Sometimes people are just looking for a little paint to finish a small project, like a cubby house. (A lady at a garage sale bought six different pots to paint all her kitchen cupboards a rainbow!) If they do not sell, take to an appropriate rubbish facility – not down the drain!

Put out flyscreens, fence palings and scrap metal (though this may go to a dealer for a better price.) It will reduce the amount you need to remove later.

Fuel tanks on garden and hobby equipment must be empty for transport.

Congratulations! You've done it! The whole house is sorted. You are now in touch with all those little treasures that had been hidden waiting for rediscovery. The hardest job is over! For now, relax and have a short break, we can start the next part tomorrow!

You have sorted the objects that are important to you. You selected them from the original jumble as necessary. Do you like what you see? With less clutter and more free space, a move may not be necessary!
The money you make in selling those unwanted chattels can go towards making your living space more personal and practical. It may even partly fund the move itself.

Change the furniture around and experiment with cushions, colour and common sense! There are lots of storage options available and books abound to encourage improved arrangement of your treasures.
For those moving on, consider the savings you have made by reducing the volume of goods to be shifted!

Disposing of your excess riches

L ook at all of the 'Selling' goods. Where was it all hiding? Make a list. It will sort out the categories you have. Decide on a **realistic** price for each article; remember that these items are **used.** (Roughly half to one third of retail depending on the condition is a good estimate.)

Item	Description	Price	Min Price	Sale Price

Example of list

The list will keep you focused. Keep in mind what you are trying to achieve. Write down the lowest price you are prepared to accept. You do not have to give it away for free. However, holding resolutely to a higher price may mean that it does not sell at all.

Your selling options are numerous, depending on the type of goods to be removed. For antiques and items of special interest, consider antique dealers and specialised auctions (in major cities for optimum prices.) For clothing, consignment shops sell good work and evening wear. Scrap metal recyclers buy metals containing precious elements.
Second hand dealers will come to you and pay for all of your wares as a 'job lot.' Keep in mind they are buying to 'on sell' – they are trying to get the best price too. Negotiate to a closing offer . Remember the final decision is yours.

Charitable organisations appreciate items that are in good saleable condition. Books, games and hobby materials are often well received at a retirement village or educational facility.

Market stalls and garage sales (see more information below,) newspaper advertisements and bulletin boards are other options. Internet sites for items of value are popular too. The telephone book or internet will help with places to advertise or market your wares.

The aim is to get the rid of as many of your excess goods as possible. If you are able to make some money in the process, you will be in a better position to move forward to your new life.

Begin to sell your goods as soon as practicable. Realistically, the earlier you start the better!

All the items have to be presented to buyers in their best possible condition. A light dusting or gentle wash will make them more eye-catching. If you are unsure of how to clean an item, obtain advice **before** you immerse that bright red lampshade in hot water! If necessary put it out for sale as it is. When someone shows interest, make them aware that it simply needs a clean. This will deter them from trying to talk you down in price, due to dirty condition.

The Market Sale

Some points to consider for a Market Stall:

- Which market place? Some are art and crafts; some for antiques, others more of a flea market. (Visit and decide which best suits your needs – resist the urge to buy – remember you are looking to offload possessions not gain new ones!)
- What fees are applicable?
- What are the opening hours of the site?
- How early can you be there prior to public access?
- Usual crowd numbers?
- Are there items that you are not allowed to sell? For example you may not be allowed to compete with regular stalls selling produce or plants.
- Do they have tables for hire?
- Exactly how big is your piece of ground?
- Can your car and trailer stay with you or must they be parked away and by what time?
- What weather conditions would cause the event to be cancelled?
- Can you choose which stall you want or do regulars get first bid?
- Are there toilet facilities nearby?
- Take someone with you to assist. They must be able to bargain with customers, without giving the goods away for nothing. You will be able to take a break when things slow down as someone will be minding the stall.
- Plan the layout of your stall the night before. Start to set up as soon as you arrive. Time is of the essence. One person to arrange work surfaces whilst the other unpacks the goods. Aim to place your boxes only once.
- You will need a torch, tools, tying materials and sheets to cover tables. If you will be setting up on a cold and dark morning, dress in layers. As it warms up you can adjust.
- You will need bags and wrapping material, a pen and markers, note paper and cardboard for signage. Keep your List handy, but out of sight of customers. Note on it (during slow periods) what has sold. It will give a ballpark value of your proceeds without visibly counting.

- **Be prepared for the Traders!** They will crowd you as you set up (even help to unpack if you are not quick enough!). Stand your ground. Ask them to leave if necessary.
- Know your list. The traders are looking for items to fill their own stalls. If you feel that something is of value, stick to your guns. You may get your price (or close to it) when the public arrives. Should it still be unsold at the end of the day, maybe the trader will buy it from you then!
- Greet your customers! Make them feel welcome. Often people will buy something if you have a rapport with them!
- Place bright or eye catching items towards the back. People will be drawn by them and will need to walk past your other merchandise.
- Your space should allow people to move through easily. You need **good visibility** of all your wares; when busy, little things can go into pockets unnoticed.
- Some people will not browse a stall if they are the only one. When activities are quiet, take turns with your helper to 'browse' and rearrange merchandise. As new shoppers arrive, take an interest in them.
- Have a 'float' consisting of small notes and coins. (Keep a few larger notes in case you need to get more change or someone presents a LARGE note.) Keep all money in a bag around your waist. Discreetly move some into a hidden pocket or another bag at quiet times. Be aware of those around you when away from the stall.
- Note the body language of people as they pay you. Check that they give legal tender, in **your** currency. Markets and sales can be an easy target for 'play' money.
- Take care as you give change. Ensure that notes are not stuck together.
- Prepare simple snacks and a drink. They must not be messy and able to be eaten in small pieces. The minute you take a bite, someone is going to ask a question! Take a chair, hat and sunscreen; you could be outside for a long time.
- Keep topics of conversation general. With too much information some people may conclude that you will accept any price, just to get rid of your goods. Don't be offended if people offer ridiculous prices. They are testing you! Smile, and ignore them.
- **Do not let people rush you.** If you are speaking with a customer, another may butt in trying to get you flustered! Ask them to wait a moment or excuse yourself from the first. (They are hoping that you will simply say the first price that comes to mind and they will get a bargain. Keep an eye on the original customer too in case it was a ruse to hide a 'sleight of hand') Consult your list – and add little – if they still want the gem, they will haggle!
- Place a box of small toys on the floor. It will be your child magnet! What parent or grandparent has the heart to refuse a child a 10 cent toy?!
- A clothes stand is very useful to display clothes and other long articles, like posters. (Other stall holders have tried to buy mine numerous times!)
- Weather can change quickly. Be prepared. If the wind is strong, much of your merchandise will end up in a heap on the floor. Have some plastic covers in case of inclement weather. A constant mist is worse than a passing shower!

A Garage Sale:

- Check with your local Council or authority about street advertising restrictions. Put a sign at the local shops and one at your driveway for passing traffic.
- Set up the night before. Arrange the 'furniture' to best suit your space. Step back and pretend you are a customer. As the sun rises and the day improves, you can move your sale outside to give browsers more room.
- Make sure the pathway to your sale is clear of any obstructions and accessible for people with wheelchairs, prams, and wheelbarrows!
- Just because you say 8am, do not think people will not arrive earlier! If you advertised in the paper, the traders will have been up early working out which sales to attend. They will knock on your door; ring your telephone (if advertised) and generally try to get you to open up as early as possible. **Remember it is your sale!**
- Have someone to help. They can act as runner; when you need something from indoors or need help to carry out a purchase to someone's car. They can take money from one customer whilst you deal with another.
- Group items according to price – when a crowd arrives, people can see for themselves. You are free to converse and negotiate on items for a sale.
- Can you reach the item at the back of the table without knocking over others?
- Have a bag for money – lots of small denominations; early customers often do not have change. (Some use this as a bargaining tool, hoping for a better price rounded to the next lowest note.)
- **Lock your house and areas of the garage that are not part of the sale!**
- Make sure those items NOT for sale, are well covered. Some people will poke around anyway, so make sure your assistant knows what is for sale and what is not!
- If someone is really interested in something, talk to them! Most people expect prices to be flexible – you get to decide how much.
- Ask parents to keep an eye on their children. If something gets broken, do not let them just walk away. You are a 'store' and your merchandise has value.

Once the sale has ended

Be careful how you store the takings. You have advertised a sale. People expect money to be in the house. When depositing it at the bank, take someone with you and be discreet.

Don't forget to take down ALL of your signs. It is annoying to drive past a sign only to read that the sale was last week! You may also be fined.
Tomorrow, should there be anything left; you will need to think about how you want to dispose of it.

For the items you let fate decide on, think how you feel about each one. Would you have really missed it had it sold? Maybe you do not need to keep it after all! Choose a selection and put these with your treasured possessions.

Have an early night! Treat yourself a little – it has been a long day!

The next day

Go and take a look at what is left. Ideally the garage or trailer is completely empty!
If it is all going to charity, go and make the call to your favourite. If they will pick up the load let them know what sort of goods you have and roughly how much. They may have to make a few pickups or deliveries on the way. Please make sure that the goods are accessible, as they will not have a lot of time to sort out the good from the bad. They will let you know if they cannot take items – they have guidelines for what is suitable and what is not. Charities are not garbage dumps!

Other places to consider donating to: Retirement villages, refuges, volunteer organisations or educational facilities. Ask around, somebody may be able to use what you are prepared to throw away!

Other Matters

Financial planning

So far you have taken stock of all your material possessions. You have pared them down and removed all the excess you can bear to part with. Now you need to consider your financial possessions. Your options will depend on your circumstances, ambitions, health and age until retirement (whether you expect that to be 30 or 60!)

Can the money you made from selling your riches, pay off excess bills or help to reduce others? Has removing the clutter opened up a space in your home from which you can now earn an income (bylaws permitting?)

There are Professional associations and good reference books available that can help you to make decisions to move closer to and maybe exceed your financial ambitions.

If you are moving:-

* How is the property/rental market in your area?
* Can you afford to keep the residence and rent it out?
* Will the rent you receive cover the mortgage payments?
* Do you need to repaint or do repairs in advance of your departure?
* Would refinancing give you more options? The equity in your current home may improve your ability to purchase your new abode.
* Interview rental agents from different companies. Make yourself a list of questions, and write down their answers. They want your business; you are in a position to negotiate some of the terms.
* Ask renters and landlords who they are represented by. Some act better for the owner, some the tenant. Your choice must be someone you are comfortable with. A relative may offer to look after your investment, but consider how they would react to a call at 2 am to fix a broken pipe. An agent is being paid to deal with this and has a list of contacts for repairs and maintenance.
* Selling the house outright may take time. Investigate options; whether you sell privately, with an agent or at auction, as early as possible. (It is wise to keep an eye on house prices even if you are settled. It will prevent you overcapitalising with renovations that may not be popular in your area.)
* If the negotiations stall, see if the agent will negotiate on their commission.
* What are house prices like in your new neighbourhood?
* Speak with your Financial Advisor and Taxation Consultant. They may suggest a plan to allocate your assets to gain maximum benefit from your investments. Consider all decisions without pressure and with care. Take time to read paperwork carefully.

Wills and Powers of Attorney

Consider your Will.

- When was your **current** one last updated?
- In all the sorting - have you removed an item that was previously mentioned? Did you find an item you had forgotten about that needs to be bequeathed?
- Has your family grown or changed?
- Have your wishes changed?
- Speak with your Solicitor or obtain a Will Kit **now**. Leaving it until later, may cause it to be overlooked again.

Do you have a Power of Attorney? It is an important document that allows another person to act on your behalf. There are various types that allow for varying degrees of control over your affairs.
The decision to appoint someone to this responsibility needs to be made with great care. Consultation with a Legal expert is needed as there are a number of stipulations and limitations possible.

Make copies of your important papers and seal them in an envelope. Place them in a safe deposit box and leave the key with someone you trust.

---

*These two documents need to be revised regularly to ensure
they accurately reflect your future wishes.*

Electoral Records and Voting

Ensure your electoral records are current. If moving, the Electoral Commission or Vote records department can update your records and advise new electorate details. If going overseas, find out the procedure should you need to vote whilst away. Your Consulate Representatives may provide facilities to allow voting.

Personal Insurance

Your premiums are based on risk factors associated with your current job. With a change in workplace or job description, the calculations may alter. To ensure your cover is maintained, you need to advise of any change in your usual work duties.

For example, if you change from primarily office duties, to spending time on the manufacturing floor. Your new job title and description will be very important. A change in name from Office Manager to Plant Manager could mean that your profile is now one of greater risk.

Home duties are seen as a greater risk than office duties. Your risk profile will increase. Your premium may rise accordingly.

If in doubt about your situation, seek professional advice.
Ask Questions and read the fine print!

Moving House

The de-clutter process was essentially personal. As you sifted through the riches in your home, you were reminded about people, places and things of the past.

Now it is time to look towards the future.

A new opportunity awaits and it entails a change of address. It may be personal preference, an employment choice or due to a health issue.
What do you think about it?

If you are not happy, try to work out why this is so.

* Has this been your home for many years?
* Are family nearby?
* Is long term employment guaranteed at the new site?

There will be sadness and some regrets. Take time to address these issues. A more suitable climate may give better health. Friends and family may be able to visit. Ask your employer for assurances in writing as to your future.

This change might improve your financial circumstances. A new home may cost less, have less maintenance or gardening. Spare funds can be used for travel or retirement. The whole world is out there waiting for exploration!

The process of moving house holds true, regardless of your destination. An international move is simply a move a lot further away! You will have a few more points to note and tasks to do, but at the end of the day, you will simply be setting up house once again.

The more planning you are able to do prior to the removal of your furniture; the better you will cope with changes as they occur. There may be mishaps, forgotten tasks or breakages. Sometimes problems cannot be avoided. Do not let them take over. Once all is complete, take time to ponder how you will do things differently next time!

Moving house is a great time to establish new guidelines for family routines. A child old enough to choose their own bedroom is old enough to get their dirty clothes to the wash basket! If you have always wanted to do a course of study – **plan it into your new routine.** You are not bound by how your house ran before. Try a new hobby, learn new skills, sit and enjoy some solitude as the world around you hurries past. Each new locale is a source of inspiration!

If you are moving directly from one house to another, the 'Long store' and 'Living' piles made earlier may seem to be one and the same. Both piles will end up in your new home. However, by separating them, you have chosen those items that are used infrequently and so not needed as soon as you are settled.

If your move is of a temporary nature, that is, you are being transferred for few months or years and will then return to your abode, your plan will be a little different. Priority in packing will be given to items of significance rather than those more sentimental in nature.

If the move involves hiring a moving van (either self move or professional,) consider the costs involved in the 'excess baggage.' You may need to hire a bigger truck, requiring a special driver's licence, more fuel and larger space for parking and loading. Remember the heavier the truck, the less likely you will be able to park in the driveway of either home!

The absolute final decision about your packing will need to be made just prior to the arrival of the 'removalists'. Until then, you are free to add to (but preferably not take from!) your 'Selling' pile. If an opportunity arises that would enable you to sell for a good price something that you have kept, consider your options.

Professional companies often charge by cubic metre of boxes packed or total weight shipped. Once they start to pack your belongings, you may be astonished at the volume of your goods. Few items will be in each box, as they try to ensure that all of your possessions arrive in pre-packing condition.

If you have a professional move, check if you are able to pack **anything** yourself. You may find that their insurance policy will not cover those boxes.

Some items cannot be moved or stored. For example, open foodstuffs, flammable materials or objects. If in doubt, ask! Moving companies will have their list. Customs and Quarantine Departments can also assist.

Storage costs can mount up very quickly, especially when the time period is more than one year. If you are moving overseas to see the sights and experience a new culture, think about how useful your possessions will be. Would it be easier to sell up most and start again?

The Personal Effects List

Whilst you are still in the 'de-clutter and sort' frame of mind, I suggest that you make another list. (Having made one for the selling process, you are now skilled for this task!)

This is your record of all furniture and other items that cannot be packed into boxes. If you have time you can make a list of the smaller things too, but they will not be listed individually on the removal manifest.

Design a sheet either in a notebook or on a computer. (Once again remember to print it off before the computer gets packed away!) Make three copies – one for your records, the others for moving and resettling days.

Item	Size	Condition	Dismantle	Move	Sell	Notes
		E/VG/G/P/VP	Y/N	Y/N	Y/N	

Example of Sheet

Abbreviations: Excellent, Very good, Good, Poor or Very poor, Yes or No. A space for notes is useful to remind you of specific needs. For example: antique, fragile, needs repair or extra heavy. Look at each piece carefully. Any scratches, rust or discolouration will degrade the rating that can be given.

Write this list **before** you contact a removal company or hire a truck. It will help you to work out how BIG a truck you will need! It will also make you aware of ALL the things that need to be shifted. (Oversize or awkward shaped and heavy items may require a bigger truck. Extra man power to move them may also need to be arranged.)
Include pianos, lamp stands, lengths of timber and bicycles – **everything** you intend to take with you.

Go through each room, including the garage and shed. If there are things under the house or in the attic bring them out. Bring items home from storage at friends' places or professional lockups.

For pianos, antiques and fragile pieces; make sure that the successful removal company is **aware** of any special care required. Individual frames or boxes may need to be built in which to house items. Extra padding to reduce rubbing or vibration damage during transport may be needed.

Once complete, put the three items of the list copies in your Essential box.

Organising your thoughts

The **first items** you need are:

a) Your **Super Luck Box**
b) **Essentials boxes**
c) A notebook. It needs to be empty (you will soon fill it up!) Small enough to take with you whenever you go, this notebook will become a friend. Give it a name – For example 'Homer' - (Think of it as one of your children or pets!)

The shorter the time frame, the more organised you will have to be. An international move in six weeks is not impossible! You are going to have numerous tasks to do at the same time. A plan of attack is most important.

Spend time working out:

- What needs to be done and in what order
- Whether you have people who can help.
- Can you afford to get some jobs done for you: for example, the final house cleaning and/or garden tidy?

In books, pamphlets or on the internet, you will find timelines for moving. These work well when time is not pressing. However, not everyone has this luxury. Read through them for hints and suggestions for your own lists.

With planning, the process is more productive.

Homer

It's time to start making notes if you have not already.

Leave the first page blank for important dates and phone numbers. They will be at easy reach when needed.

Common thoughts include: 'Why do we have all this stuff anyway?!' (For the literary amongst us – a good essay topic!)

Inside, record:

- **All** the little thoughts that cross your mind – emotive or practical – a form of stress relief!
- Any questions you have.
- Useful points of advice you receive from others.

- Phone numbers – both for now and at your new location.
- Answers you receive from businesses – (name of the person you spoke to, the date and time.)
- **Your** new contact details.
- Any dates or appointments you need to remember.
- Lists of any items you need to find specifically – paperwork or items to be returned.

Homer becomes your **Reference Book**. Carry it with you so that all the information for this move or cleanout is with you. It frees your mind for more important matters.

The move itself is rarely the only issue on your mind. You are thinking about your job, family, social life and even just some quiet time. Homer is a tool that allows you to rest. In the night, if you think of something, get up and write it down, then go back to sleep! You haven't forgotten about it. You have done something with the concern and it will be dealt with at a more appropriate time. NO! The shops are not open at 2am! You need your rest more than anything else!

Grab your telephone books, computer with internet access (if you are proficient—now is not the time to learn!), the telephone, a non alcoholic beverage and a few nice biscuits or a piece of fruit. Now the fun begins!

Stick a calendar on the inside cover. It will help when making appointments.

As you go through these points below, start to make notes and/or appointments. Note down or deal with tasks as they come to you. Annotate the listing clearly to remind yourself the task has been done. Make sure it stays readable!

Colour code tasks to do in one day or week to make them easier to find amongst all your notes.
Some hints to get you started.

Important phone numbers and contact details: Red
Day/Week/Month One: Blue
Day/Week/Month Two: Green
Day/Week/Month Three: Orange
Emotional thoughts: Purple
Helpful hints and comments: Black

Pencil in some free time for yourself and your family!

The aim is to deal with each task as few times as possible. If you need to make an appointment or hand in some papers after initial contact with an organisation or company, set this down as a new entry.

Review progress daily and weekly. **Initial** bookings need to be arranged as soon as possible. Ask each business if they need any paperwork from you to complete the appointment.

Start with the information that you **know**. This will help you to focus. Write the day **and** date; dates will fly by quickly as moving day approaches. Hopefully you will know a date of departure and where you are moving to!

How will you and your possessions travel? Are there any restrictions on what you can take?

What season are you moving to? Even across the country, temperature and humidity can vary greatly. Watch the weather maps that appear on TV, in the newspaper or on the internet. This information will assist as you pack your bags.

Try to visit many businesses in one day rather than a separate trip to each business. You will save much time in finding car parks or waiting for buses. Any paperwork that you receive from organisations needs to be brought home for perusal. Then you can make notes or a list of questions, fill in details and find relevant information required.
A lot of the jobs that need attention must wait until close to moving day, as you may need specific information to complete paperwork.

Pets

Your animals will need travel papers. Is a new medication routine needed? If a quarantine period is necessary, investigate starting this process while you are still here. You may be able to visit and reduce your time apart. Your pet will join you at your new location sooner. (This may be delayed if you are not going to your final accommodation for some time.)

Your wallet

Clear a space on the table (or floor if necessary!) and empty out your wallet, briefcase or handbag. Now you know why your shoulder is drooping and your back is out of alignment!

Take out all of the rubbish – scraps of old lolly wrappers, used bus tickets, receipts (should be with your filing) and old tissues. Gather up all the small change. Look at each business and credit card in turn. Will you need them at your new location? Could they be stored in a card holder for reference? Which ones can you cancel? (Add to your 'to do' list.)

Make a list of all those reference numbers found on cards and membership papers. (This list should be put in your **Essential box.**)
Make sure all companies are on your Change of Address list **(Essential box.)**

Change of Address Form

Fill in a Change of Address form available at the Post Office. Nominate for whom it applies and the duration of the redirect. As you inform companies, make a note of when advised and the date the new address is used. Start the redirect a few days before your departure to ensure no mail is left in your mailbox.

Passports

Are children free to travel, or do you need to sort out custody issues? Do not assume this will be a formality.

Where is your passport? Is it valid? If it will expire whilst you are overseas, enquire how to renew it. Is the document itself in **good** condition? Visas are needed. There have been recent important changes to travel documentation procedures. The time frame for replacement can be lengthy. Do not leave it too long to get started!

Are children to be on your passport or their own? Is anyone entitled to multiple passports? Be aware that each country has its own regulations regarding work, national service and entitlements. Research this option carefully.

Save spare passport photos. You may need to fill in a form or need to replace a document. They must be recent – children change, you have shaved your beard or dyed your hair! (Keep one in your wallet or purse for identification.)

Doctors and Dentists

No matter where you live, these days finding medical practitioners can be difficult. Waiting lists are common. If you are not going to be living close enough to use them again, ask for your records to be put into their archives. This may open up a space for another family just like yours – on the move and looking for a new start!

Overseas travel often requires vaccinations. Some courses take a number of weeks to complete. They may make you unwell for a few days. Young children may be irritable and their arm may be sore.
When was your last Tetanus shot? Updating this now will give you a reference point for the future.

To leave the country, you need to show that you are in good general health and will not be a burden on your intended countries health system. Forms need to be completed and signed by the medical officer. See if your surgery has sufficient forms for your family, or take them with you. Fill in as much as you can before you arrive at your appointment. **Note how long the clearance certificates are valid for.** It is a waste of money and time to have to redo these should they expire prior to departure. For dental checks, allow time in case you need a filling or other work to be done.

Surgeries and clinics are very busy. Last minute appointments are not always possible. Advise the surgery why the appointment is needed.

Obtain copies of medical notes and X-rays.
Ask your Pharmacy for a copy of your record. Give a copy to your new Dispensary. This information will ensure your pharmaceutical history is maintained.

When moving from one State to another, check with your private Medical Insurer about changes to your cover. Individual States set their own reimbursement limits for each type of treatment covered by their policy (For example dental, podiatry and dietician cover.)

If moving overseas, ask if it would be prudent to suspend your Insurance. You may need a letter from work to confirm your impending transfer. Find out what wording they require. Make sure you understand **all** implications should you think of suspending or cancelling your policy.

If you decide to suspend your Medical Insurance, as you will be unable to access its facilities, check **thoroughly** the implications of this decision. How is a condition that develops whilst the policy is under suspension to be dealt with? You may become pregnant; have accidents or a familial illness start to show itself.
When you return, will you be able to claim for expenses relating to this condition at time in the future?

Banks

Find out from your bank if you will be disadvantaged by having your account originate in another State. An account established in one State will still be liable for that State's taxes even though you now reside in a new State where they do not apply. You may decide to leave the account idle (but subject to account keeping fees,) or open a new account in your new State.

For overseas travellers, ask your bank:

- Can you access your account from abroad?
- What fees will apply?
- How long will it take for transfers?
- What happens to money sent or fees paid if the transfer is unsuccessful?
- Is there a more economical way to transfer money from one bank to another?
- Is internet banking an option?
- What fees are applicable for currency changes?

A bank needs multiple forms of identification to satisfy security requirements.

Once settled in your new country, arrange for a local currency credit card. Your card from home will charge fees for converting purchases from one currency to another. For example, purchases bought in Canadian Dollars will then be converted to American Dollars. Another conversion is required to convert the bill to your home currency. Read carefully any terms and conditions.

Vehicles

Think about your new home.

How many cars do you **need**? Will there be space for all your vehicles? Include the bicycle, boat, car, trailer, motorbike, campervan, motor home and snow mobile! Special permission is often required for oversized vehicles. There are restrictions on how many spaces you can occupy in your street or garage.

Leasing can be more economical if your mileage requirements are minimal. Consider selling two cars and buying one that better suits your future plans. (Are there motorbikes in the family? – let them stay – a rider's happiness is important!)

If you have a boat, is there a usable body of water close enough to enjoy regularly? Hiring one for a holiday now and then could be more practical. Think about the costs of wear and tear, maintenance, registration, insurance and storage.

Investigate the local transport system. Take a trip and see if you like it – not all of us are comfortable leaving the driving to others!
Where does the route go? Will the need to change bus/trains too often, make them impractical to use? How long will it take to get to the shops or work? See if there are express services to get to your destination.

If you are having your car transported by car carrier, take clear photos to show the condition (interior and exterior) prior to uplift. Give a copy of the prints to the movers and keep a copy for your records. (Ask the mover to sign that he has received them.) Remove any unnecessary items from within the vehicle. A condition report will be filled out by the carrier, check the 'damage' noted.

If your decision is to sell your vehicle, consider that out of season it can take longer to find a buyer. Who wants to buy a boat when it is too rainy or cold to go out?

You need to advertise as soon as possible.

Be careful with your reason for selling. Nobody likes to pay more than they have to. Negotiation is expected. The more time you have to sell, the better your position. You don't have to take the first offer made. Think carefully though before rejecting an offer – will you realistically get more by waiting? Think about the cost of advertising and the worry about not selling?

Cars, motorbikes and trailers, will need a certificate of roadworthiness before you can sell them. (Check with your local fuel station to see if they issue them.) These certificates are only valid for a short time. Then they need to be applied for again.

A fee is payable each time. If maintenance or repairs are necessary, negotiate with the buyer on the price.

Ask friends and neighbours where they look for vehicles. A particular market or news media may be more popular.
Visit local car markets and take note of the age and types of stock on display.

- Would your car look out of place here?
- Are there too many similar?
- Could you sell your bike or boat here too?
- Do you park and remain with the vehicle; or leave them in a lot and have the attendant contact you when an interested party arrives?
- Will you be able to take the vehicle out before the end of the day or weekend?
- How many weeks must be paid in advance – is there a refund if the vehicle sells quickly?
- Does the auction house nearby get good results?
- Visit an auction. Are the prices near your expectations? Terms and conditions need to be considered.

Vehicles need to be clean and polished. What accessories or special features will you include in your advertising to draw in the buyers?
Dig out all the maintenance records for the vehicle to pass onto the new owner. Have you found any password or code numbers needed? Locate all the keys including spares.

If the vehicle is to be taken for a test, ensure your Insurance policy is current and allows this activity. Take care when allowing someone to test the vehicle alone. What security can be exchanged? (**Note they may not have visited you in their own vehicle.**) Could you follow them?

Once you settle on a price, sign a written contract with the buyer. State the price and when it will be paid. Do not hand over the vehicle until the money is definitely in your bank account. Enquire with your financial institution whether a fast clearance on a cheque is worthwhile.

An example to get you thinking: Trying to sell his car, the owner let the buyer know that he was moving. The buyer assured him that he wanted the car, so the owner held off other prospects. When the day came for payment, the buyer said that he only had funds less than agreed. Diplomatic words eventually made the situation right, but it was a stressful time for the owner as his plane trip was fast approaching!

Consider how you will finish your numerous tasks without your vehicle after it sells. If necessary can you hire a car to tide you over?

Car Insurance.

Be VERY careful when transferring cover from one State to another. Some companies will close the original policy and then start a new one for your new address. This **will** disrupt your years of service! It may have taken just a few minutes to effect the change; however, the computer will only see that the policy is NEW! A problem arises when you need to prove your 'No claim Bonus' status. Without producing old policy documents, you may find that your rating is a lot worse than it was before the changeover occurred.

This changeover of details is best done in person at a branch if nearby, so that the Customer Service Officer can sight any relevant documents.

Policy premiums will vary from one area to another, based on their statistics of claim. (Sometimes it will be a pleasant surprise – other times it will be a shock! – You may need to pay more to maintain suitable coverage.)

Obtain a transcript of your Driving Licence details. Blemishes will show up, but you would have had to inform future registries and Insurance companies of many of these anyway. If you have not lived in a State or Province very long; obtain records from your previous location as well.

Automobile Club membership.

Ask if your cover can be transferred. Not all are affiliated and it is not **automatic** for them to accept another organisation's customers. If you will be without a vehicle for a limited period of time, and have a continuous membership of five years or more; see if you can change to a lower membership status and maintain your years of service. Future discounts available to loyal longstanding customers will be lost if your coverage is cancelled and started again. You can upgrade your subscription when you return.

International Driver's Licences are obtainable from Automobile Organisations. You will need a passport photo. They are valid for one year. Ask if they can be renewed from out of the country, if necessary. Check that it will be a valid licence in the countries through which you intend to travel.

A Licence to drive in one country does not automatically entitle you to one in another.

Borrowed items

Now is the time to gather all those books, cassettes, CDs, videos, tools and toys that you have lent. Some may feign possession, but be patient! Hopefully you had your name on them when lent out. They will come back eventually!

Any Library books and other items have to go back. Make sure that you send the school library books to the school and the Community Library books to the community library. Overdue fees may result if there are delays due to a mix up. If you aren't sure if you have any outstanding loans, check with the institution concerned. If you cannot find the books outstanding, let them know that you are aware of the loss, and are looking for them. Many people will sympathise with you about the upheaval a move creates. If you show that you are making an effort, they may give you more time before penalties apply.

Hand in your old library cards if you are definitely finished with them. It will be one less card in your wallet and ties up a loose end.

Antiques and other old furniture

Understand that not all of your goods are in perfect condition. Unless they are new, they have experienced life's knocks and bumps! This highlights the importance of the De-clutter stage. Your Personal Effects List should have noted pieces of furniture that need repair.

Antiques are unique in their own right. They have a history - through your family or just as a special item that gives you pleasure to have around.

Sleepless nights are the last thing you need during a move. The underlying stress of not knowing if your furniture survived the rigours of a long journey can be very taxing.

Here are some aspects to help you decide if a piece of furniture should be included in this move.

- Would it be better to start afresh at your new location?
- Seeing a space unencumbered with old memories may allow you to experiment with new styles or colours.
- Are you sure that your well worn dining suite will fit into that kitchen /dining area?
- Are you tired of looking at the same furniture?

The decision can be difficult to make, especially if you have an attachment.

Investigate as many options as possible.

If, for example, a cabinet needs some restoration:

- How recent was the last professional valuation? The monetary value alone of the piece may not warrant a great expense for repair.
- Is there a local antique tradesperson able to do the work?
- Could it be sold at a good price in a local market or would you have to take it to a bigger city? Would the piece survive such a journey?
- Is there a Specialist Auction house that deals with pieces of this type? Would you get a satisfactory price?
- The removalist chosen needs to be knowledgeable of how to treat such distinctive pieces. To have a pane of glass broken or leg cracked or destroyed can be distressing.
- Do not let the Movers bully you into leaving the pieces behind. Being told that, 'in their opinion the piece will probably not survive the trip anyway', does little to inspire confidence! If they have real concerns, they should be discussed prior to moving day. If you have concerns, insist they visit your home and have a look at the furniture **before** they accept the job.
- Be present when they are loading and padding the piece onto the truck. If damage occurs, ask to see it. Contact the main removalist company to let them know what has happened.

Perishables

This includes items in the Kitchen pantry, Refrigerator, Freezer, Bathroom and Laundry.

You need to reduce stores. For a local move, this is not so critical, as you can move these items yourself. Removalists will not move any opened containers.

Those small guest soaps that you souvenired on your last holiday! Take them to your new place as a starter kit. Use up first, those items that take up the most space. Two or three normal cakes of soap are heavier and more bulky than half a dozen small ones! You will replenish these items when you have settled – for now you simply have to get them there.

Laundry powder – in preparation for an impending move, purchase a smaller box. It may cost a little more for the convenience, but there will be less wastage. 'Spring-clean' over time, so that by the day of the final clean up, most of the grime has already been removed. Keep out all those cleaning products for your last sweep through.

If you are organising someone to do this task, start asking around for references. Your Real Estate agent should have people they can recommend. Go through the house and show them what it is you want done. Be specific; your idea of scrub clean and theirs may vary!

Think of possible adjustments that will be necessary to the cleaning plan should the weather prevent some of the jobs from being completed on time. Your agent may be able to arrange times for the services to be finished. This is most important for carpet cleaning as you need ventilation for the carpets to dry properly.

In the kitchen, you get to be creative. Look through your receipe books to find an **edible** use for the stock you have! Internet search engines are useful. Access sites where, by entering a few ingredients you will be offered a menu of dishes to try. Hopefully some of them will be tasty!

Most jars (preferably not glass) or tins that are unopened **can** be moved. Concentrate on using up what would otherwise need to be thrown out or passed on.

If there is time, make up some meals that can be frozen for those busy nights when you won't want to cook. A family day of cooking can make this chore a lot more fun!

If you have more than one fridge or freezer, condense your foodstuffs and turn these appliances off as they empty. Clean them and leave slightly ajar to dry out. If closed they will smell!

These appliances need to be empty, clean and dry **twenty four hours** before the removalists arrive.

Children enjoy coming home to find that mum has baked **another** cake or their favourite biscuits, just to use up some of the flour and sugar stockpile. Make some fun dough. (Receipe found in many books.) It will keep the younger ones busy.

Children's activity: When moving day is very close, make up a tray of food items that you will not finish. Into small containers put, for example, flour, salt, cocoa, cereal, tomato sauce, spices and the like. Into old drink containers, add food colourings to water (hot or cold) to make different 'ingredients'. Give the children mixing bowls and cooking implements so that they can enjoy 'cooking' their own creations.

Children five years and older, can have a small amount of Bicarbonate of Soda and an amount of Vinegar (separate containers.) Show them how they react – it's the 'Fizzle factor!'

This activity is best done outside on a grassy area.

WARNING: The vinegar will kill grass if it is concentrated in one spot! Dig a hole and ask the budding chefs to put their finished creations in there. It will keep them amused for quite a while. A bucket of warm water with detergent added will encourage them to clean up after they have finished, as part of the game. (Children can have just as much fun with the water as the food kitchen!)

Planning for Disaster!

I am not trying to frighten or stop you from going ahead with your plans. However, it is prudent to consider what options are available should something drastic happen.

A few possibilities: serious illness or accident, goods in transit destroyed, future home unhabitable.

As you start to make plans, ask your Insurance Company and or Removalist what would happen should the worst occur. Make sure they can explain **fully** the extent to which assistance will be given.

Some questions:

- When does their cover start?
- What does it cover? (Items and situations)
- What doesn't it cover? (Items and situations)
- After what period of time will they step in to assist?
- For what length of time will compensation be paid?
- How do you access funds for immediate purchases if necessary?

Nobody ever expects these things to happen, which is why you need to spend some time **now** considering their possibility.
These events occur without warning and often there is nothing that could have been done to prevent them.

Some real life examples:

Moving interstate, a moving van full of household goods rolled over in a traffic accident destroying everything. The young family were moving to a large city where they knew nobody. A hard start to a new life, but they got on with living and started again.

In another case, a family had exchanged contracts and accepted keys to their new home. Preparations to move were in order. Whilst showing friends around in advance, they found to their horror that some vital plumbing (located in a separate facility to the house) was missing! An inspection had been carried out by a professional building inspector. He had not checked this structure on the property as it was not in his checklist.

Their move was planned for the following week. With a one week old baby in the family, not being able to use a single tap in the house was going to pose a problem! Fortunately, they were able to extend the rental contract at the house they were in, for an extra few days whilst repairs were carried out. The furniture was able to be delivered. When they moved in, a lot of the chaos was already sorted.

A final example: A retired couple were to move into a home unit. The week before, however, it was destroyed by fire. Another unit was found nearby and they were able to move without major delay. (The second unit suited them better than the first would have. Maybe fate simply found a way to steer them in a better direction!)

You will need to think about alternative housing. Will it be covered by Insurance? What standard of housing will be provided and for how long? Will you be able to break a rental contract without penalty once a permanent home is found?

If your children were to attend a local school and this turn of events means that you will be living away from the area temporarily, let the school know as soon as possible. It would be a shame to have children start at one school for a short time, only to have to start again once you settle.

Furniture deliveries can pose a major headache. You will need to research alternative 'holding' depots into which your goods can be offloaded until a solution is found.

- Will the second move of your possessions be covered by your policy? (From Storage to Home)
- How long in advance will you need to book the truck?
- Who will pay the storage costs?
- If friends or relatives offer to temporarily store your goods, look carefully at the space.
- Is it well ventilated, open to the weather or a potential haven for vermin?
- How long will you be able to leave your contents there before relationships are strained?
- Will your contents insurance or their house policy cover the risk should their house burn down whilst all your belongings are there? (Insurance policies can be VERY specific.)

You need to ensure that you have taken all precautions possible
to avoid damage to your property.

Major illness at any time can throw a family into difficulty. Trying to spend time at hospitals, continuing to work and take care of other family members is a job best not done alone. There are people available to assist in many situations, often all you need to do is ask.

Nobody can or will want to step in and take over all the worries you now have. At best, they may enable you to get a few hours of exhausted sleep. Urgent or occasional childcare or respite for you and your family may be available. Offers of meals or basic house keeping may come. Accept them gracefully. (There may be an occasion for you to repay the favour one day.)

Hospitals may have lists of organisations which you can call for assistance. Local government departments and Consulates or High Commissions can also be good sources of information.

Another thought. Work or a change in lifestyle has given you the chance to live elsewhere. You have rented out your home for a set period. However, the experience is not what had been envisioned. You now wish to return early. Rental agreements are legal and binding. When negotiating the terms and conditions, investigate wording or length of contract options. This may make it harder to find a tenant as everybody likes security. Living from week to week, not knowing if the lease is to be cancelled can strain relations quickly.

If funds are available, open an emergency bank account. It will allow you to return to your previous location and rent another property until the lease can be terminated.

The main aim of this forward planning is that it gives you options. When stressed, seeing a way out can be difficult. Facing these challenges hypothetically will broaden your focus. At the new location, you will become more aware of what facilities it has to offer.

Education

Advise schools or educational facilities of your impending move. Obtain a report on your children's progress. Subject guidelines will assist their move from one class to another, hopefully without having to repeat a full class year. Teachers at the new college will want to know what your children have been doing and in what areas they may need some extra help.

Intending students will have to show that their childhood immunisations are up to date. If there are ethical or medical reasons for not completing them, have an official document to show the relevant educational board.

Library cards and school enrolment will need an official receipt with your new home address on it – a post box address is not normally sufficient. Check if the chosen school is obliged to accept enrolments from within a local geographic area only.

Loose ends

- Make arrangements for final reading of meters and/or disconnection of cable TV, internet, gas, electricity, water, telephone and newspaper delivery services. Ask if there are any security deposits to be refunded to you.
- Pick up the dry cleaning or other items left for repair. Also remember to finalise any lay-away outstanding.
- Go and get those Lottery and raffle tickets from your **Essential** box. Check these <u>before</u> you leave! Some are not able to be checked across the border. You will want to ensure your winnings find you! If you **are** fortunate enough to have a win, a cheque may take **some weeks** to be sent out. Make sure that you give a 'reliable' address for delivery! (A trusted relative or friend who could deposit it into your account when it arrives.)
- Find all the memberships and subscriptions you have. Think about which you really enjoy or use. Some publications are found in local libraries. (You may have to wait in turn for the latest copy.)
- Update or obtain valuation certificates for jewellery (including wedding rings and watches,) art work or other treasures. Shop around for a suitable valuer. It may take some days for the documents to be ready for collection. A cost may be involved. (For International moves, your Insurance Company may ask for a copy for their records.)
- If you are moving yourself, arrange for packing materials. Check the local telephone book for companies that 'hire' them – they sell them to you and then if not too knocked around they buy them back. Local newspapers often contain advertisements of people who have boxes they no longer need. (Look over them carefully for insects.) Get creative with portable storage units you have.

- Organise accommodation for any nights once the packing boxes start to get filled. Consider the time enroute and temporary housing until your new home is ready.
- Investigate Travel Insurance for time in transit. Illness, accident or transport delays can wreak havoc. (When travelling for work, some insurance may not cover you if you have a holiday prior to starting work at your new location.)
- Find out if your new home will be cleaned prior to your moving day. Your agent should know or be able to arrange this.
- Ensure you have electricity and water connections on the day your furniture and boxes arrive! A connected telephone is useful. Television and Internet services can be delayed until you have had a chance to shop around. (If you are able to connect with the same company as your previous address, you may not need to provide a new deposit. Your previous account numbers may be all that are required.)
- Ask your contents insurer, about coverage during the move of goods transferred and those stored. They will have rules and restrictions. You cannot have your goods insured by two companies at the same time; (that is, the moving company and your personal insurance policies.)
- If your home is now to be a rental property, your Insurance policy will need to reflect this change.
- Arrange for carpets to be cleaned and appropriate treatment if pets have resided indoors.

Your last task each night is to make a list of jobs to be tackled the next day. If you wait until breakfast, you will lose precious hours as you search for paperwork or take time to drop off goods that other members of the household could have taken with them.

For your notes.

Moving with children

Children of all ages are affected by moving house. Their way to show this is as individual as they are. They may go off their food, wet the bed, become more mischievous, become aggressive or reclusive or simply rebel against any suggestion you give. Have patience! You need to consider their viewpoint and come to a solution.

If they are under two, all they see is that you are too busy, tired or stressed to play their favourite game one hundred times!

Under five years of age, they can see what is going on, but will not necessarily understand all the implications that will follow. If you are always too busy, younger children can fear that you may forget them and leave them behind!

Find ways to include them in the process. Give them a box or a drawer and some items to pack – (items that are staying behind are ideal.) At such a young age, they like to imitate the actions of their parents and siblings. By distracting them, you are able to get on with tasks that need to be done.

Over five, their reactions will be determined by their age. School friends may be lost if you move too far to still attend the same school. They may be attached to their backyard cubby house or have to give up extra curricular activities. They may just want to complain because they can!

Make them aware as early as possible about the move. Show them where you are moving to – either by visiting the place or with photographs or a map. Assure them they have important roles to play. They can help sort out their possessions and clothes. They can assist the 'packers' to pack their belongings. Appoint them as messengers. (Younger children would appreciate a special sticker or badge to wear.) Give them a clipboard and write something for them to pass on to another person.

If these tasks are too 'juvenile' for your brood, make them responsible for something! They can tick off the boxes as they are being loaded into the truck. You need someone to feed the troops throughout the day. Entertaining younger siblings, running errands, putting items into your car – anything that stops you from having to leave the job you are trying to complete. Once all is done, a treat of a movie or special activity may help to smooth over the hurt feelings.

A few days before

Find small totes that each child can pack to take with them. (The rest of their toys will be in boxes.) Make sure that there are quiet and noisy activities. Encourage the items to be small so more fit in! A pack of cards – (matching games, Snap!, building card houses,) a notebook and markers for their ideas and feelings (a page covered with dark black scribble could well be the confusion or anger they are feeling.) Small cars, dolls and a favourite cuddly are all welcome.

Into your personal bags, put some new toys. Finger puppets take no space and are great for airplanes or confined spaces. If you give them a toy that needs more than one player, ensure that there is someone who will have the time. Don't forget some spare batteries. Check with your carrier what is allowed in hand luggage.

Make sure you know what each child has packed! Children's safety scissors are considered a potential threat too. They will be confiscated on check-in. Think carefully about your handbag. Nail files, pocket knives, calculators (you may need to show how to use them,) knitting or sewing implements can be confiscated. These items should be packed into your baggage compartment luggage.

When packing, any items to be packed into your personal luggage need to be separated from the rest of your possessions. Use an empty room and mark it clearly as not part of the removalist's responsibility. Make sure you have sufficient space for this volume of goods. Once the packers leave, there is no where for any excess to go.

You need to empty your wash basket. The washing machine will need 48 hours to dry out. Once you have completed the last load disconnect the power. Get a bucket **before** you undo the hoses, as there will be a quantity of water still in them.

Any clothes from now on can be hand washed – provided you are sure they will dry – do not put wet washing in a suitcase! It will weigh more and it will smell! If necessary, a trip to the local Laundromat will keep the pile from getting out of control!

Ferret out those clothes that can be washed and worn without an iron – one less task that will require your attention.

The night before the move

Tomorrow will be a very tiring day. There may be some confusion, decisions to be made on the spot and people everywhere. Knowing this in advance, you can start to prepare now. If others are to help, decide what job they are going to do. You need to be the overseer. If there is a problem, they need to come to you **before** the work starts. Don't get bogged down on one task; other work may be overlooked or not done to your satisfaction.

Types of duties:

- Dismantling furniture
- Liaising with removalists
- Keeping children occupied
- Keeping the troops fed and watered
- Making sure every room is emptied – Have someone who does not live there check each room. Make sure they look for pictures on walls, items in drawers and cupboards. They are there, but you may not 'see' them. In your mind's eye they are part of the wall. Don't forget the bathroom scales that you have stubbed your toes on, oh, so many times!)
- Find your Personal Effects List

Wrap private items before the onset of the 'moving crew'. It may take a while to live down the smirks if they find your 'special' night wear! They can be left in packaging until everybody has left!
Keep one set of old clothing for each member of the family. These clothes are for wearing as you prepare to leave. They will be thrown out at the end of the moving day. (Clothes that are getting too small or scruffy are ideal.)

For local and long distance car moves; keep your first aid kit, Essential and Special boxes handy, in case you need them quickly. For International moves, these will all need to be packed away. You need to take sufficient paperwork to cover education, work and medical records and insurance details in your carry on luggage.

Prepare yourself some snacks that you can eat whilst on the go. If you are able, ask a neighbour if you can use their kitchen. Your kettle will have been packed along with cups and the like. Keep out a few rolls of toilet paper; they are always a handy addition to your suitcase, no matter how far you move!

Neighbours may surprise you and turn up with afternoon tea in hand. As the truck is being packed, you get the chance to catch your breath. Sit quietly and get your thoughts back into order.

Day of moving

The day has come for the last of the furniture to go. Your brain starts realise that this is no longer going to be home. The rooms will look different and sound hollow. Memories of times past may start to fill your mind. You will wonder if you are doing the right thing. Take heart – a whole new life awaits, lots of surprises good and bad, new opportunities and memories to be made.

Prepare your strategy for the actual day. Keep garbage bags for rubbish, Homer and a pen, paper for notes, mobile phone charged up, phone books handy and a sense of humour! You will be tested more than once today and starting with a happy disposition certainly makes things easier!

Young children will be excitable today. They may also be lost. Their whole life is being turned upside down. All their familiar things are disappearing into boxes. A strange truck is taking them all away. Let them see the boxes being numbered to go into the truck.

Make sure their favourite toy is in a safe place. Show them where they are in your car or luggage. Place them there before the movers come!

The removal process can be dangerous as boxes and furniture are being shifted out and onto trucks. Little feet and fingers can easily be crushed if they are not seen amongst the chaos.

If possible, arrange for the younger ones to be somewhere else whilst the truck is being packed. Try to arrange a meal at a family restaurant with indoor play equipment or a park to use the swings or kick a ball. They need to be away from the action for a while to process all that is happening. A chance to run around, have time to eat and ask questions will help them to adjust.

Mark the oven door with a 'Do not remove' sign. This may deter an earnest helper from packing the shelves from within. (You feel a little sheepish when you have to send them back to the new resident!)

Remember to leave with the oven any baking dishes that came with it. Leave the instruction manual where it will be found – or if renting out the premises, give it to the real estate agent. They can arrange copies for the tenants as required. (This applies to any and all appliances that are staying with the house. For example, Hot water service, Stove, Refrigerator, Washing Machine and Dryer, Heating and/or Cooling units, Microwave, Special light fixtures and Alarm panels.)

If you have names of paint colours, spare carpet remnants or tiles, leave them for the new owner (or advise the agent where they will be stored.) Your new address has no use for them. The new residents will appreciate your thoughtfulness.

If you have knowledge of underground pipes or other essential services, take a picture of the area and label it clearly for the new owner. It may save them expensive repairs in the future when they are revamping the space.

Empty the garbage bins and clean all those coffee cups and dishes from breakfast. It can be rather unpleasant opening up a box of kitchen items that have been in storage for some time to find mouldy cups and rubbish that should never have been included in the inventory!

If self moving, have some order to the way you pack and unpack the boxes. For each room, number the boxes according to what will be needed straight away. For example, those items that have been stored in the wardrobe can be numbered '20.' You will know that those boxes can be left until later to be unpacked. Those numbered '1 through 5 etc' should contain tonight's bedding and towels, toilet paper, kitchenware to make a simple meal, and any school or work books that will be necessary to start straight away. Some children's toys would also be handy.

Once these are transferred, you can prepare snacks and get a good night's sleep whilst the changeover occurs. Send back a box of sandwiches and drinks to your old home to feed the workers. When people are hungry, if you present them with food, few will get fussy. Lots of water, coffee and tea are important to stop dehydration. Alcohol is not recommended, as people may attempt to lift weights that are in excess of their usual abilities. Breakages are also highly possible.

The prospect of a party after the move may be enough to keep them motivated.

You will know what day the house will be empty and so can plan down to the last detail. You may be living between houses with some items in both as you slowly empty one and fill the other. (It may be wise to have someone stay in each house whilst they are being transformed.)

Ensure that each box is properly packed. Mix up an assortment of light and heavy items so each box does not get too heavy. Ensure that all items are well padded. The aim is to ensure that nothing can shift around in the box during the transport stage. If there is a potential for leakage, wrap and then place in plastic bag. Secure well with tape.

Make sure boxes are assembled properly. Mark **clearly** those that need to be placed on top of the stacks. Ensure small items are wrapped in bright paper and labelled. Tape them inside the bigger item where possible so that assembly can take place on arrival. Ensure each box is marked on the outside with a general description of its contents or which room it came from.

Ideally for close moves, have people at both houses. With enough friends and family, it can be a tiring but most rewarding day. Those at the old house pack and transport the contents to the new house. At the new house the people on hand unpack and arrange the furniture to make it ready for living once more. One big advantage to this method is that you can recycle your packing materials.

Set up the children's rooms on arrival. Let them sort their things. They need to know where they will be sleeping and that their favourite toys have been located. You might be lucky and get them to lie down. They don't have to sleep, just take time to get used to the change of house.

The Inventory Sheets

This very important document will be compiled by a removalist company as your boxes and furniture are removed from your home and packed onto the truck. It is their record of what they have handled. It serves as the official record when your goods go to storage or are passed on for delivery. It is also used to verify the condition of any item should a claim be lodged for damage noticed after delivery. Take time to read through it carefully. You will need to sign each page. Do not be hassled just to sign them because the truck wants to leave.

Assign someone to go through your Personal Effects list and the inventory sheets. As each piece is located use a highlight pen to mark it off.
Check the descriptive marks given on the inventory sheets. Ask your helper to advise you if there is a discrepancy. If there is a great variation on a particular item, ask the removalists to explain their appraisal.

This will be a tedious process as the lists will not be in the same order. Great care will be needed to match up the right descriptions.
Ensure they also advise if something appears on one list and not the other. Make sure that **all items** are listed. Some may be put onto the truck as an afterthought but not added to the inventory. If they do not arrive at the delivery address, there is little that can be done.) Without a notation on the sheets at the time of uplift, it is very difficult to prove your claim later.

Some Scenarios to consider!

Moving Coordinators are available to plan and execute a move if you prefer. They do charge for the services provided, but leave you free to pick up your hat and walk away from the chaos. At your new abode, a turn of the key will reveal a home tastefully decorated and filled with your possessions.

They will have guidelines for each type of move and will adapt the most suitable to your requirements.

With gathered experience, they will deal with changes as they happen. They also have the advantage of 'distance' – they are not attached to the items to be displaced. When **you** are planning the event, each decision is personal. It is you that has no bed for the night, it is your picture that got left behind or broken.

They are another option to consider.

If your budget will only stretch as far as having a removal company to change your household from one address to another, then one of the following plans will suit you.

Activity Four:

Think about how you would adjust the flow of boxes and tonight's restful slumber if the pace of the transformation speeds up! Write down the plan of attack for each in Homer. As the situation intensifies or problems arise, upgrade your plan.

Scenario One: Your entire house lot is being transferred direct from one house to another. This would suit a home unit or small house lot. The truck arrives in the morning. The boxes are packed and loaded onto the truck. As soon as the truck is full, you leave the house and head for your new life! (If the distance is great you need to book overnight accommodation.)

Regardless of the distance to be travelled, emphasise that all is to be packed securely – just because you are moving down the street does not mean that things cannot be broken!
The truck arrives and drops off your goods in your new home. Everything is unboxed, furniture is reassembled and you can make afternoon tea on your favourite plates!

Scenario Two: The packing process is staggered. This suits a 'temporary' move where you will return to your home one day. You are only taking to your new home what you consider necessary for the time you are to be there. Furniture may be shipped or sent to long store. The costs involved in shipping furniture are great. Suitable fixtures may be provided to suit the climate or living standard. Renting furnished lodgings is also an alternative.

The goods going with you will be removed first, so that they are available upon your arrival. There may be a day or two before the remainder of your possessions are packed up ready for storage.
If you have sufficient towels, blankets and cups (essentially your settling kit,) then you can continue to sleep, wash and cook in familiar surroundings.

When the removalists come, all that is left in the house will be packed and taken to long term storage. These items will not be accessible until you return home.

Scenario Three: In this dream sequence, the packing of all your goods is to occur on one day and the removal to take place on the next. This is a straight forward house to house transaction.
The truck arrives. The Removalists head off into different parts of your home and begin the job of wrapping treasures and stacking boxes.

These goods may travel by road, rail, ship or aircraft depending on the destination. Time delays can occur until you are reunited with your boxes. If necessary they will be put into short term storage until you find your next home.

All is progressing nicely. By mid-morning the boxes of packed items are growing and the cupboards are looking pretty empty.
How much they can complete in one day will depend on the size of the job and the time they arrived. As the sun sinks in the sky, they bid their adieu. With almost empty cupboards, you await the return of the removalist van on the morrow to finish packing and load up all that you own. Realistically, you can still sleep and wash in your home, and go out to eat.

The items to be packed into suitcases, the cars and the trailer are all you will be left to live with. (An assumption has been made that you are going to a furnished dwelling for the interim.) Whilst the truck is being filled tomorrow, you will calmly pack, clean out the rooms, remove any extraneous rubbish from inside your yard perimeter and spend time saying goodbye to the neighbours. You assume you will have time tomorrow to calmly pack these whilst the truck is filled. A leisurely night awaits you as you contemplate the next day!

Scenario four: Not for the faint hearted! This is real action packed drama.

We set the scene the same as sequence three. BUT – the previous evening (before the packers arrive,) you took time to dismantle the beds and tables, disconnect and pack the Television (left the box open,) empty the cupboards to a central location and generally simplified the packing.

The truck arrives. The workmen have a look around and are impressed! Appreciating all the assistance you have given them, the removalists start to pressure you that they want to pack and remove everything in one day!

This is to Scenario four!

For your scheduling this means that you are out of house a day early. No beds, no towels, no coffee cups – time to go!
Call for a break in activities.

Find those items that you wanted to take directly with you. Pack them now!

(If work commitments mean your significant other has already left to start their new employment, remember that **you** are in charge. You are in the middle of the boxes and people and can see exactly what is happening. From a distance, it is easy to assume that the process is occurring as described in a textbook!)

If you get to a point where there are people wanting to ask you instructions all at the same time; call a halt to all actions. Give each person a number and ask them to wait. (Seriously!) Deal with each in turn and give them your attention. You will think more calmly and clearly.

There are advantages to this scenario, however without forethought; it can be quite a jarring suggestion.

You need to arrange the night's accommodation. Whether at a friend's home or a motel, at least you know you have somewhere to sleep, whatever happens!

Realistically, if your contract allows, you may say, 'NO - see you tomorrow!' However, when the paper starts to fly and the rooms start to empty, it is easy to get caught up in the excitement. This scenario needs at least two able bodied people on your side of the equation. One person needs to finalise the packing of your personal luggage, whilst the other supervises the removalists and generally keeps things humming!

Consider the prospect: Two half days of planned chaos have now joined to become one VERY LONG day of activity. Long summer days of good weather and long twilight can make this a 'doable' option. Mid-Winter days of below zero temperature and early darkness, falling precipitation, the need for a replacement removalist van and young children hungry, bored and wanting to help, leave you wondering about your sanity to attempt this move at all!!

You thought you had time to pack, say a final farewell to neighbours and give the rooms a general if not good clean out. Rubbish that needs removed will now have to be done by someone else. Those disconnections and final readings will go ahead as scheduled (weeks ago) as it is too late to change them.

Alter your thought process. Think of the **extra day as a bonus**. All that needed to be done has been. The time is completely free! Be a tourist in your city one last day, spend some time being pampered at a spa – all those aches and pains need some attention. If you are to travel by car, stop at some of the sights along the way that otherwise would just have been blurs in the rear view mirror!

Take time to catch up with all that is happening. Do something totally unrelated to the move. A loud sing-a-long, a family game of soccer – anything that allows you to vent some of the emotions you have kept in check.

Your brain needs some down time. If it goes into overload, staying focused for the next part of the adventure will become more difficult.

Activity Five: Practice now. How would you handle this situation?
Your helper has walked in and asked for assistance. At the same time one of the removalists is asking what name to put to an item of furniture. The Real Estate Agent happens to drop by and see if they can show a potential client through **NOW**, and your spouse is on the phone wanting to know how things are going?!

Removalists

If you are being moved by a professional company, find out their usual plan of action. Your destination, length of stay and who is paying for the move will all be factored into how the move is to be carried out.

Your move will fit into one of the scenarios described above.
Find out the name of the persons that will be attending your home. Ask for identification when they arrive, if you feel the need. You should feel comfortable trusting these people with your goods.

People laughed when they saw an episode on TV of a removal van parked at a house in a suburban street. It showed a good natured bystander even help to load a rug onto the truck. It was not until the owners came home did people realise that they were not moving at all!

Make sure you know who is removing your worldly goods!

A major removalist organisation will request an inventory from you. It may be sent via the internet or fax, or they will send someone out to discern the volume of your freight and any special articles of note.
(Make sure you show them ALL items. Remind yourself to look under the house and all through the garage and shed.)

They then tender your job through their contracted moving companies. The successful contractor will contact you and let you know what dates they have planned for your consignment.

A packing team may have numerous houses to complete in a week. By considering the urgency of the order, the size and location of each job in relation to the others, they plan their schedule. Sometimes it can be simpler to pack each location and then pick up in turn. If the jobs are separated by distance, completing one job at a time is more efficient. If one job is able to be completed sooner than expected, they can get a start on the next. The team begins their time off when the jobs are complete, not when the clock says 5pm!

For small moves and those of a local nature, your goods should be handled by one packing team in entirety.

For long distance and moves that require storage time before final delivery, goods can be uplifted by one company and then transported by another to their final destination. Finding the responsible party should there be damage or breakage can be difficult. You will have to establish when it occurred. You may not have a say in which company does the work, and sometimes there can be a problem getting a company to deliver goods that they have not packed. They, too, are conscious of possible damage to items in transit.

Ask if a removal company will bring things out from their storage spaces or are you required to do this. Also ask if they will put items back under the house – for example - at the delivery address – they may stipulate that
they deliver to a flat surface only.

BEFORE the removalists begin, make sure they understand how you want your special possessions packed. If necessary have one overseer for each packer. This may seem harsh. However, it is impossible for you to keep check on three packers in three rooms at the same time. As you are checking on one, another can have two or three boxes packed.

Specific instructions need to be given. If necessary, ask them not to close the boxes that will contain your most precious pieces until you have inspected them. All the assurances in the world count for nothing, when you find at your final destination that the request for careful wrapping had been disregarded and your valuable china now lies in pieces at the bottom of a packing box.

Vigilance by you whilst the packing is being done is the key.

If you have the original packing box for a valuable item, for example, a Television; let the removalist put it back in. If **you** do it, they will mark the box as '**Packed by owner**' and it will not be covered by their Insurance! They may allow you to pack it, but leave the box open for their inspection. Ensure the Inventory Sheets have been marked correctly. (See heading.)

PBR = Packed by Removalist / PBO= Packed by Owner

If you do not like the way something is being packed, SPEAK UP! The foreperson should have introduced their team upon arrival at your home. If you have concerns about the people packing or any damage that occurs, let the foreperson know. If you are not happy with their response, contact the Major organisation NOW! They need to know. Their reputation is at stake, as these contractors are acting on their behalf.

Do not wait until all the boxes are on the truck before you complain about how poorly Aunt Molly's vase was taken care of!

If damage or breakages do occur, make sure it is noted on the inventory sheets.

Please do not think I am against removalist companies. The job they do is difficult, as they try to fit all of your riches into a truck so they arrive safely. They are not emotionally attached and are aware that you are. In their hands it is a vase, but to you it is a lasting memory of your favourite aunt who has passed on.

Once all the furniture is gone.

You may be a little stiff and sore. Children may be a little confused as to where all the furniture is. The truck has left. The house is bare. Walk around in each room and say goodbye. The memories will stay with you. The house was and is simply a shell which facilitated their creation.

Accept that this is the beginning of a new adventure!

If necessary, arrange for the final cleaning of your old home to be done. Remove any rubbish and empty the garbage bins.

Leave a forwarding address with someone you trust. (Get them to number each piece of mail they readdress – it will help you keep track of them.) There may be the odd piece of correspondence that you have overlooked. Leave a note for the new owners or tenants informing what to do with any mail that arrives. Let them know what day the garbage is collected and where the 'good take away' shops are! Any recent bus timetables or other local knowledge will be welcome.

Once you have arrived at your sleeping quarters gather everybody together. With all in clean clothing, celebrate as you toss your old clothes into the garbage. Take time to remember the good and bad times you had in your last home. Acknowledge that being sad is okay. Moving house is traumatic, and each time is different.
It is a challenge for anybody regardless of age or how many times they have moved before. There will be some unknowns to be worked out, but as a family, most issues can be overcome. Often all it takes is time.

The unknown awaits. It has been a very long day.

International moves

These require some modification to the planning listed above. You will need to be more ruthless with what you take – space and weight costs money!

You need to gather as much information as possible before you start to pack. Each country of destination will have different challenges for you. (Look in your local library or check the internet for information on local culture and customs.)

- How are you and your goods going to get there?
- How long will your cargo take to arrive?
- Are you going to temporary accommodation, for example, a hotel for a while, while you find your new home?
- What will you need as soon as you get there?
- Can you buy new items cheaper than the cost of transporting your old ones?
- Is the climate quite different, will your present clothes suit your requirements?
- For electrical items, will your articles work properly on the new power source? Will you need to purchase transformers?
- What furnishings will be available in your temporary living place? (Homer.)
- Where you are travelling to and into what season?

What to take

For those leaving the country for a limited time, you will have two moves to make. One for the goods to go into storage and the other for the goods to go with you. The removal company will want an estimate of the volume of items for each. Mark out a space. Anything put inside this area, is to take with you. Lay it all out in rows so that it is all clearly visible. Try to start this as early as possible. Add some items that remind you of home. Pictures are good to brighten a dull day. Realise that you will gain possessions. People in other countries are interested in where you have come from. Many have not travelled to foreign shores, but have seen them on television. Limit books if you can. They are heavy and take up a lot of room. Calendars are a lightweight alternative to show pictures of home.

(Delicate figurines and odd shaped fragile treasures will have to be carefully wrapped. Get someone to make a wooden box into which fragile or difficult to wrap items may be placed. It will make them more robust and better able to survive the process.)

The removal company will appreciate that you are organised. They will be able to assess quickly what packing materials to send. Resist the temptation to fill them! Clothing is the only item that you should personally need to pack.

Start your suitcases at the same time. What you pack will depend on what will be available when you arrive. Do not just throw everything in; you need to ensure that every piece can be coordinated with at least two others. What you take will have to do until you move into your new home. Pack clothing for each family member in each bag. If each person has their own case, should one be lost, then they will have only the shirt on their back to wear!

If you are not staying in initial accommodation too long, pack complete outfits for the family in each case. Only open one at a time. All the dirty clothes go back into this one and the rest of your clothes stay fresh.

Find a way to make your cases look distinctive amongst the hundreds of other bags on your airplane or train. Make a list in Homer of the contents of each bag. If one is lost or destroyed, you will be able to estimate quickly the total cost of your loss.

Pack your medical and education records, work orders (if applicable) and address book in your carry on luggage. In your notebook, you should have important phone contact numbers and other pertinent information to tide you over till your chattels arrive.

If there is a particular chocolate bar, or bottle of wine that you simply cannot live without, check if you will be able to take a personal quantity with you. It will act as a 'pick me up' whilst you settle into new surroundings. Some items will not be practical, they may melt or packaging may open, so check with the Customs Department to see what restrictions are applicable.

For guitars or other musical instruments, skis, a pram or car seats, ensure they are well protected. Wrap in plastic to protect from rain and snow. Make sure you cushion any protruding fittings that may get broken or damage other luggage. Mark your possessions as distinctly as possible.

Long Distance Travel

Your mode of transport (bus, airplane, ship or train) and the makeup of your family will affect the way you prepare for the expedition.
Know where your travel documents and passports are.

Minimum hand luggage is best. Domestic and International limits vary in weight and size. Pack for the lightest limit – there is not always the space for leniency. **Be aware of the contents of each case.** Pack a complete change of clothing for each family member. Disposable underwear is available at Pharmacies and on the internet. At your destination, with a change of clothes, clean teeth and face washed, you will start the next part of your adventure 'fresh'.

Think about the climate at your destination. Will you need your big heavy winter coat for stop overs, or will you be able to wait until you collect your suitcases?

For those moving from extreme cold to a nice sunny climate, make the clothing kept out to sustain you for the last few days of your stay 'disposable.' To pack snow suits and mittens into minimal luggage allowances when you are going to 'lands of endless sunshine' is a waste. Donate them to a local charity. They will be appreciated.
As you dress for your journey, note in Homer what each member of your party is wearing. Make sure you note which leg of travel these clothes are for!

Check the minimum amount of time required to be in the terminal prior to travel. If arriving by taxi or car, factor in time for heavy traffic or a flat tyre!

If you are having people to see you off, have them meet you at the airport **early** (or possibly for a meal the night before.)
A thorough Customs and security check takes time. They are necessary. Patience and courtesy to the officers will help. Allow plenty of time. There are many passengers to be processed and all have departure times to meet!
Slip-on shoes are more practical as you may have to remove them for inspection.
Keep a pen handy to fill in forms.
Advise Customs of any medications you are carrying.
Declare your Duty Free purchases.

Children will have to pass through security devices alone. Show them in advance what they will have to do. Have an adult go through first for them to meet.

Organise someone to collect your bags off the security point.
Be prepared in case someone is stopped for further checking!
The sensitivity of scanners varies. You may pass straight through at one departure point, but be stopped at another wearing the same outfit.

For special needs, diet, bassinettes or wheelchairs advise the airline as early as possible and confirm these requests a few days prior to travel. If you are a nervous flier, let staff know. They can provide reassurance and strategies to help. Advise if children are travelling unaccompanied. Ensure the child is aware of the person to collect them. Put a photo of this person with the child's papers for added verification.

Once you have checked through your luggage and said good bye to any well wishers, make your way to the departure gate. Spend as much time as practical walking around.
During travel, you will spend a lot of time seated. Spend time wearing young children out! Keep a close eye on them. It is very easy to lose them in a constant stream of people. Walk up and down in an area away from other passengers. Let them dance to music; look out at the planes and vehicles used to service them. See if they can see your luggage as it is taken out to be loaded. If possible, use the conveniences in the terminal. Aircraft or bus toilets are a little cramped if you have to assist a youngster. The more tired you can make them; the longer they may sit 'quiet' once boarding starts!

When you hear the announcement, 'passengers with young children and those needing assistance', make your way to the gate. Have your boarding passes (and passports) out and ready for processing. Ensure the children have their bags, and all the toys that they pulled out.

Once on board, spend time, showing them where facilities are and how to clip and unclip their safety belt. If flying, children under two years may be able to use a safety belt that attaches to yours whilst they sit on your lap. The flight attendant can advise if they are available onboard.

The length of the trip will determine how to entertain your party. Try to stop the little ones from emptying their toy bags. One toy out and one back in will keep some order. Make food times as leisurely as possible. (Bring a few small snacks with you just in case there is little onboard to tempt a fussy eater.) Older children may enjoy the movies or music provided. Check if they can use their computer games.

If you need to take medication before, during or after a flight, make sure you have it in your personal luggage. Any papers that identify the 'patient', the dose and the medical practitioner who prescribed it must be with you. If delays to travel cause a problem to your medical routine (and the consequences are potentially serious) inform a crew member as soon as possible. They will have more options available to assist, if they can arrange for your needs before your condition is critical.

Before boarding aircraft, turn off your mobile phone and other electronic devices.

Delays to travel

Delays can occur for many reasons. Aircraft and trains are being scheduled from cities and countries near and far. Weather conditions can differ greatly from departure point to destination. Mechanical concerns can ground an aircraft or train carriage at any stage. They are a necessary precaution and are not the fault of the service officers! It costs a great deal in customer confidence and money to have an aircraft or locomotive off the schedule. A lot of shuffling has to occur, as the carrier reconfigures crew (and their allowable time limits of work) to get passengers and their luggage to their destinations or connecting travel plans. They do not always have a spare engine nearby. To change the travel plan of another aircraft or train may solve your dilemma, but cause hardship for others.

Patience is the key. If possible, send a spokesperson to enquire about the travel arrangements for a group. Ensure that children are lightly fed and occupied.

If you are given a form by the flight attendant, fill it in before you land. The more prepared you are, the less stressed you will be as all the passengers converge on the exits to make their way to the luggage chute!

Once you arrive, collect all your pieces of luggage. Ensure they are **yours**! Gather all your items and then check over them carefully. If anything is broken or torn or missing, inform the Baggage Collection Office. Calmly explain the problem. For a suitcase that is completely destroyed, give them a list of the contents. You may want to inform your travel insurance operator as well. If a piece is missing, they will want to know your flight details. They may offer to send it on to your forwarding address later.

You may be a little sleepy after sitting and eating, the children may be either asleep or hyped up for sitting too long. Try to keep them away from the luggage chute or line of suitcases.

An example: A young family arrived at their home airport after a holiday. Their suitcase was on the baggage carousel but their child's car seat was not. They could not leave the airport. (They had driven to the airport as it was some distance from their home.) The airline explained that some of the baggage had to be left behind at the departure point and that it had been put on the next flight out. (At small airports there can be a priority list for certain cargo.) After a delay of an hour, the missing items were located and they were on their way. Apologies were made by the airline and updates given to assure the family of the arrival time of the aircraft.

Once you reach your accommodation establish your regular routine as soon as possible – in the time zone you are now in! Jet lag can be unsettling and time is the cure. (They are devices and medicinal preparations available; ask at your local Pharmacy or Health Practitioner for suggestions.) Children may find it hard to go to bed whilst the sun is still up. If it is daytime, go out and look around. If the weather precludes a stroll, find an indoor activity to suit your family. Nothing too intense, somewhere that allows you to burn off some of those calories you gained whilst travelling. (For some, long periods of sitting can cause constipation. A walk will assist in resetting your system. Ensure you can locate a bathroom in quickly – just in case!)

If you are initially in a hotel or motel, the less time you spend indoors the better! Pick up tourist brochures and a local paper. Ask at reception. In between your efforts to settle into new employment, find your new home, a vehicle and schools; make time to sightsee. Once you are settled, you will always find other commitments that take precedence. Talk with the locals and find out what the attractions are for the current season. It will help to 'break the ice' in meeting people.

Keep a map with you. When walking around it can be easy to become disorientated. Before setting out, try to find some landmarks from your map to look for. Be confident whilst out in the street. Holding a map or hesitating could make you a target for opportunists looking to take advantage of your situation.

Give yourself time to think by window shopping, stopping for a coffee break or visiting a library or museum.

Deep Vein Thrombosis – (DVT)

This medical condition has gained a lot of attention. It can affect people of all ages and health. With increased security measures, walking around inside an aircraft may not be as freely permitted as in times past. Airlines usually have some information available on exercises that can be done whilst seated. If you have concerns, speak with your Medical Practitioner whilst you are having your medical examinations.

Medical needs

You need to find out if you can take your specific medicines into your new country of residence. Some have very strict laws. Customs may be able to give guidance in this matter. For specific medicines, obtain a letter from your Doctor that details the active chemical ingredient and its concentration. Also include any other information that will correctly identify this prescription. Dosages and brand names may vary or change. Do not assume that you will be able to find your usual brand of headache tablets or antiseptic lotion.

Take a prescription for your glasses or contact lenses. Ensure you know where you have put your spare pair.

It can be frustrating when you want a particular tried and tested remedy, but have trouble conveying your needs to the local people. Describe symptoms rather than asking for a particular brand of medicine. Often going back to basics will help. Keep an eye on the condition in case the symptoms become more severe.

Another consideration is allergies.
Make sure you carry sufficient information at all times regarding medicines or substances that react unfavourably with your body. Language difficulties can exacerbate this further. Ensure you have the contact details of your local consulate facilities and the doctor in your **home country** that is familiar with your medical history.

If you annually suffer from Spring-time allergies in September and October, consider that across the Equator, Spring-time occurs in April and May! You may or may not suffer as in the past, as your particular irritant pollen may not be present. On the other hand, if you have never had allergies, be aware that in a new environment, there may be something new to tickle those nasal hairs!

Finding a new home

The internet is a marvellous tool. Local Libraries often have terminals available for the public to use. The staff can give guidance to get you started. With this technology, you can start your search before you leave your old home. Visit real estate offices online in your future city.

You will narrow your search very quickly. Whether by price, location or house, you can view properties quickly. As you view, have a checklist to compare each. Write down what it is that you really like. You may find a pattern emerging. Is it the garden that is drawing your eye or the view of the water out of the kitchen window?

You cannot make a definite decision about a house, until after you arrive and have had time to get to know different areas. A house can look spectacular on your computer screen, but the advertiser may have left out a view of the neighbours (true story – the neighbour was a Sewerage Treatment Plant!)

An internet search may provide information on house prices in your chosen area. An owner/ occupier history and current Rate charges of your intended home may be available. (The local Council may not give you access to this information as you are not the owner.) A local newspaper will give prices and a general description, but no background information.

Once you have an area in mind, can you take a holiday to see it for real, before you have to move? Remember that you will be a tourist. Spend some time just sitting on the park benches. Do you like the 'atmosphere'? Is the quiet comfortable, or does the noise invigorate you?

Drive around. Do you like the layout of one suburb over another? Collect tourist brochures, local newspapers and transport timetables. A street directory is most helpful. As you hear different suburbs mentioned in conversation, look them up, and find out where they are.

A real estate agent may be able to access properties of other agencies. Ask what arrangements are expected should you like a property listed elsewhere. How much commission is payable and to whom? Do you have to pay both agencies or do they split the fee? Can you negotiate on the fees?

If you are having someone else find a property for you, be exacting in the instructions. Their idea of a large backyard may not be the same as yours. Ask them to measure rooms if necessary! If the room is painted a particular colour, make sure you know what it is. 'Cream' can be anything from off white to light brown!

Photos and internet or digital pictures can have distorted colours due to screen

condition and lighting. Take colours seen as a guide only.
For Settlement proceedings, make sure that both parties are aware of the appointed date and time. Check a day or so <u>before</u> to ensure there are no misunderstandings!

If more that one person (or family) is to rent the same house, ensure that all are listed on the lease. This will ensure that all are equally responsible for any damage and expenses.

A house inspection by a reputable firm is recommended.

Enquire what exactly they inspect.

- Will every window and door be checked?
- What major and minor repairs will be necessary?
- Will they look in the roof space and under the house?
- Will they check all buildings and sheds on the property?
- What happens if you find things wrong that were overlooked?
- How will they check appliances if the power and gas are not connected?
- Do they check water (hot and cold) quality from all taps in Laundry, bathroom and kitchen?
- Are the pipes, storage tanks or hot water system full of rust? What about Solar units?
- Do the toilets work?

• They may say that they cannot be responsible for ALL doors and windows. They simply do a sample. There may be different levels of service provided according to cost. Know what you are getting for your money!
• Your Solicitor has the responsibility of doing the searches on the property. Find out as much as you can:
  - Did the house receive its Certificate of Completion when it was first built?
  - Are all Pest Treatment Services up to date and were they carried out properly?
  - What paperwork is available for the home – plans and Sewerage diagrams or any extensions or alterations?
  - Were all alterations passed by the appropriate authority?
  - What were the last Water and Services bills? Water charges may be rated per house – not on the people residing there. An owner may over subscribe the water limit to get their garden looking its best for sale! Once it is exceeded, the rate per kilolitre jumps to the higher rate as any water used is now deemed as excess. This charge is maintained for the rest of the current year. Check with the relevant State Authority as to when this expires. A change of Owner within the year **does not** necessarily start the meter reading again!

Your new home

Activity six: Welcome! Have a good look around you. Go into each room and take stock of what you see. I will give you some time...

- Did you look **up** and make sure you have light globes in each socket and that they work? Sounds silly, but there is nothing to guarantee that they will be there!
- Has the electricity been connected?
- Are smoke detectors installed and do they work?
- Do all the water taps work; and is the hot water system on?
- Telephone connections can be made with a phone call. Have you been left a telephone and telephone phone books – have you found them yet?

As your boxes are being moved into your new home, have someone check off all the item numbers on the inventory. You may need more than one person for this task if goods are going to different areas of the house. For example, some goods may go to the garage and others inside. Take note too, of the condition of each box or item. If there is obvious damage to the exterior, get the removalist in charge to observe its opening. This will remove doubt as to when the damage occurred - that is, in the removalists care or after delivery.

Check your agreement. The removalists may have been contracted to empty the boxes on arrival. If so, let them. Any breakages that occur, unless in previously noted deformed boxes, may not be accepted by their insurer if you have unpacked them.

Each box will have been packed with some layers of paper in the bottom to act as a cushion. Take out all of this paper to ensure that no small pieces of jigsaw, cabinet hardware (shelf holders) or the remote control unit to the TV have been left. Once the boxes are taken away, these gems are gone for good! Ask who is to remove the boxes from your premises and when. Some will leave this task for you and others will offer to take empty ones with them today and arrange pickup of those remaining in one week's time.

As you settle in, here are a few extra jobs you need to do.

- Change the locks. It can be hard to know how many keys were issued by the previous owner.
- Find out who installed the alarm system. Change the Master code as well as any security access codes that may be on their detail sheet.

Make it obvious new people have moved in.

A true example: Unbeknownst to the new owners, the home they had purchased had a former life as a brothel! The home was in an ordinary suburban street, with no obvious signs to give away its past!
They were noticing that cars had been slowly driving past, but did not stop. Eventually neighbours explained about the previous 'tenants.' The clues they had been finding came together into a startling picture!
A remedy was found, by allowing their children to play in the front yard (under adult supervision.) Passers by could see that the old residents were no longer there and so eventually left the home in peace. The new residents also stepped up their security measures as a precaution.

House Fairies!

They do exist! You will find them after you move in. They can hide in the smallest space and simply stare you in the face. Their job is to welcome you into their corner of the world. If you are awake early in the morning, they may have dressed your window view in a fine spray of mist so that everything glistens in the sunshine. You might find that they have provided you with the right amount of space to fit all those treasures you packed. This may seem childish, but in amongst the stress of moving, it is good to have something to make you smile. Be happy for small wins!

For children, the house fairies can get them excited about their new home. For the younger ones, before they arrive, install an inexpensive set of chairs and table. Impress on them that they are from the 'house fairies.' It will help them to forget about the confusion. Their focus is now on the present. This set will give them **their** place to eat, to draw pictures and jump their cars off.

For older children, hide a small gift under their pillows for bed time. When they 'bump' their heads, they will get a lift to know that the fairies have been watching and want to reward them for their efforts throughout the day! Those particular toys become special. It doesn't have to be anything expensive, **just unexpected.**

Take time to look around your new yard space. The whole idea is to convince your family they are not alone and that this house move was a good idea.

House escape plan

In hotel or motel rooms, the safe exit plan is displayed on the inside of the door. I hope you give it a few minutes of your time. In an emergency, you need to know instinctively where to go. A new house is very similar. You are used to the layout of your previous home.

When awoken from a deep sleep, you are most likely to automatically walk down the corridor and turn left, because that is where the door was in your old home. Now if you did that, you are likely to bump your nose on a wall that mysteriously sprung up whilst you were asleep!

Make a drawing of your new house layout. Sit down with all the family and ensure they know how to leave their rooms and where to go once outside. If your climate makes standing outside at the nearest lamp post not possible, for example, snow or heavy rain; at a time convenient, go and meet the neighbours!
Go across the road, rather than next door, in case the emergency escalates. Reciprocate the gesture. If they had not thought of making a plan, then this may give them reason to do so.

If a family member will need to break glass or climb out of a window to escape – you will need to show them how to do this safely. Make it very clear that this action is **only** to be used in an emergency!

Ensure visitors are shown their exit paths also.

Practise your plan at intervals. Ensure that children know to 'Get down low and Go, Go, Go!' as the Fire Brigade teaches.

If someone has to collect the Essential boxes or other important material, ensure they know where they are and that they can carry them. (Acknowledge, too, there are situations that will make retrieval impossible. A person's life is always more important than a box of paperwork.)

New surroundings

You have done it! The chaos is over. Boxes are unpacked and suitcases squared away.

Work is becoming more familiar. You know what bus or train to catch and you have found the best time to hit the roads to avoid the worst of the traffic jam!

Making contacts at your new job and finding your niche will take time. Enjoy the opportunity to learn new systems and methods. Quiet confidence is a better countenance. You may feel that your previous work experience is not being used to its full potential. Any efforts you make to assimilate will be appreciated. Your abilities both positive and negative will show over time.

This move may mean that you find yourself at home on a more permanent basis than you have previously experienced. It will take time to adjust. The last couple of weeks or months have been busy – much like a full time job. Now your role has changed.

It may take six months before your routine is established. If you have children of school age, the time at home will be quiet and possibly lonely. With the housework and cooking done, the day can pass very slowly.

Get out and meet people. Volunteer organisations welcome newcomers. They cover all forms of work. A few hours or a day at a time would be appreciated. Find the cause best suited to your abilities. You may try a few different places of work before you find your calling. Consider the experiences you gain along the way as part of life's mysteries! (Ask questions to ensure that you are happy with the expectations and work conditions.)

Craft, sport, studies and gardening are options to explore. The local phone book, newspaper or the internet will provide ideas. Maybe now is the time to label all those photos stored in envelopes and left in a box. Looking at all those faces, may inspire you to write your memoirs!

Make a list of all those aspiring thoughts that float through your head. Writing them down gives them credence. You may find one that stands out. Can you develop it now? Opening this window may create opportunities you did not expect.

Your children will make new friends. Encourage play dates, either at local playgrounds or at a home. Meet parents and get involved in school activities.

Ask around for babysitters. Take time out to be an adult, rather than a parent.

Meet the neighbours. They are full of local information as well as being a friend-
ly face across the fence.

With children under school age, your time will already be filled. If you are used to
having them in childcare, looking after them full time can be frustrating. See if
there are playgroups or casual care available in your area. Bus and train rides are
treats for them and a chance to get out of the house for you.

Moving without children may mean that you are alone for a lot of the day. Get out
and see what your new city has to offer. You may be able to find paid work.

If you are overseas for a limited period of time, check the viability of work. You
may have to forgo part of your income to participate in compulsory government
schemes that you may not be eligible to access during your stay in the country.
These include unemployment benefits and Retirement schemes. Check if recipro-
cal arrangements are in place with your home country.

Ensure your qualifications are valid in your new city. Some jobs require you to reg-
ister there before you can practise your trade. This includes doctors, nurses, teachers and bus drivers.
Get out and see the local sites. Maybe you can become a guide to show other new
arrivals around. Opportunities are always there; you just have to unearth them.

Find out where the local medical emergency offices are and their hours of service.
When someone in your party requires urgent attention is not the time to make
enquiries.

Visit the local hospital and find Admissions. Where do cars park? Is there a different entrance for admission during the night? How many people can enter the facility? (To reduce the risk of infecting healthy people, some hospitals allow only the
patient and a minder – other siblings or family members are to be cared for elsewhere until a diagnosis is made. You need a contingency plan for this scenario.)

If you need to make long distance telephone calls to keep in touch with friends
and loved ones, there are a number of options.

• Enquire about prepaid telephone cards. Some offer very good value. Note the
  time of day you make your calls. The number of minutes contained on the
  card can disappear at different speeds depending on whether it is used at peak
  or off peak times. (This is not always easy to define.)
• Check with local phone services as to deals or packages offered.
• Some companies have special tariffs for international calls. Any calls made
  appear on your normal telephone bill. You dial a telephone number to connect
  with their system and then dial your number.

In Conclusion

I hope reading this book has given you reasons to think seriously about your home and what it contains. Change can be hard work. If the timing is right, you may find that many of the small steps start to fall into place with little effort. Your mythical 'guardian angels' are letting you know that this move is a right decision! They may not let you know why, but go with it. Positive thoughts breed positive outcomes! The odd setback is thrown in to ensure you do not get ahead of yourself.

Take the process of moving one step at a time. It is tedious to have so much planning to do, but as with many facets of life; the best preparation makes for the best outcomes. Plans do change.

Look back at your former homes as memories, but do not compare them with the new. There will be differences, but these may be why you moved in the first place. Each new place has special qualities - you just have to find them!

Good luck. Tomorrow is another day. The sun will shine (eventually!) and the fog will clear. With your familiar cups and some ornaments around you again, the chaos will settle. Be open to opportunities as they are offered – your new world is your oyster! Live it up!

A page for your notes

Checklist of tasks

- Activity 1
- Activity 3
- Activity 5

- Activity 2
- Activity 4
- Activity 6

Sorting
- Filing Cabinet
- Bedroom 1
- Bedroom 2

- Bedroom 3
- Bedroom 4

- Clothing – Adult 1
- Clothing – Adult 2
- Clothing – Child 1

- Clothing – Child 2
- Clothing – Child 3

- The Study or Den
- The Bathroom
  Craft and Hobbies
- The Kitchen
- The Settling Kit
- Children's toys

- The Book case
- The Garage, Shed or
  Basement
- The Laundry
- Plants and Trees
- Roof spaces and under
  house

Selling - preparations for:
- Cars
- House

- Market stall
- Garage sale

Other arrangements
- Financial Planning
- Wills and Power of Attorney
- Personal Insurance
- Electoral Records and Voting

Moving House preparations
* Homer
* Personal Effects List
* Pets
* Passports
* Change of address form
* Doctors and Dentists
* Medical visits and forms
* Banks
* Removalists
* Borrowed Items
* Antiques
* Perishables
* Planning for Disaster
* Education
* Inventory
* Suitcases and hand luggage
* Travel plans
* **Free time!**

New House preparations
* Finding an agent
* Internet searches
* House Inspectors
* Moving in
* House Fairies
* House escape plans